Immune System

In Search
Of
A Court Of Law

Virgil Langley

FIRST EDITION.

Non-Fiction
Some Briefings Available at www.leafmark.com

ISBN 978-1-4303-0212-4

Published by Lulu

This book is dedicated to Bea,
For Love and Endurance,

And

To all who seek redress for injustice.

Table

Foreword

"From the moment they first contact the court system, most people who want to represent themselves, without a lawyer, encounter tremendous resistance. Within the closed universe of the courts, this bias is as pernicious as that based on race, ethnic origins or sex.

This bias exists in direct contradiction to the Supreme Court's ruling in *Faretta v. California.* that everyone has the constitutional right to proceed without counsel. The reasoning behind that decision means that the Constitution requires our justice system to be neutral towards the self-represented litigant. That in turn means that the courts must offer a level playing field for the represented and unrepresented alike, consistent with basic principles of fairness.

The Problem: Are courts really biased against self-represented litigants? Clearly so. Here are just some of the realities non-lawyers are up against when they try to use their courts:

a. Procedural requirements are often perversely difficult.

b. Strange--and unnecessary--terms are tossed about. Court jargon--should we call it lawbonics"? -- serves as a means to exclude from the courts anyone who doesn't speak the language or doesn't pay a lawyer to translate.

c. Judges and their courtroom personnel are often either condescending or downright rude.

d. Court clerks withhold information from non-lawyers that they routinely give to lawyers. If a lawyer's office calls to ask about a particular scheduling procedure, for example, the clerk provides all sorts of answers without thinking twice. But let a self-represented person ask for the same (or even much less) information, and it suddenly becomes legal advice. Many clerks' offices feel compelled to post signs saying, "We don't provide legal advice!" Most often, that means that they are unwilling to help unrepresented people get into court or respond to a lawsuit. (Imagine if IRS clerks refused to answer questions about how to file a tax return.).

e. Even if the clerk's office has a special "pro per" window, it's no guarantee of real help, or even civility. Recently I saw the clerk at such a window hand out information the way some farmers slop the pigs. When I asked whether she had volunteered for the job, she looked at me as if I were crazy.

f. County law libraries--in many states, supported by filing fees paid by non-lawyers--are operated almost exclusively for the convenience of lawyers. Non-lawyers are often made to feel distinctly unwelcome and again are visited with the "we don't provide legal advice" admonition when making a normal request for reference information.

g. People who show up without lawyers are singled out and labeled (in Latin, no less) as "pro per" or "pro se" litigants. As is frequently true with other group labels imposed on a group from outside it--"cult" and "handicapped" come to mind--these terms mask a deeper institutional bias.

Why are the courts so unfriendly to the self-represented? They weren't always that way; in the first 100 years of our history, the courts dealt equally with all comers. But in the late 19th and early 20th century, the courts came to serve the needs and interests of the legal profession, which took control of them and built a monopoly over who can appear before them as advocates.

There are probably a number of reasons why lawyers and the courts they control are biased against the self-represented. Among them are:

1. Many people could pay a lawyer but choose not to. Their choice repudiates lawyers and their "special gifts" and takes money out of lawyers' pockets.

2. Because non-lawyers are unfamiliar with court procedures that are set up by lawyers for lawyers, they tend to get in the way of smooth court administration (but no more, it should be noted, than do many lawyers).

3. People who can't afford a lawyer are a rebuke to the organized bar's monopoly over legal services, because that monopoly is morally--if not legally--justified only if the legal profession is able to provide affordable justice for all. The lawyer bias against the self-represented is a clear case of blaming the victim--even though for years, the ABA has admitted that 100 million Americans can't afford lawyers.

A number of recent studies funded by the courts and the ABA have advanced the concept of the multi-door courthouse, where courts would offer potential litigants a menu of possible solutions, many of which would not require a lawyer. This concept assumes courts want to reach out to prospective users and help them resolve their disputes in a manner appropriate to the dispute and the resources of the parties.

Unfortunately, the ideal of the multi-door courthouse is at odds with how courts traditionally operate: to support and enhance the lawyer business by making it extremely difficult to get through court without a lawyer. As long as courts are institutionally biased against creating a level playing field for the self-represented, it will make no difference how many doors a court has.

. . .Few lawyers are able or willing to come to terms with the fact that a significant portion of their livelihood is based squarely on barriers to self-representation that the courts erect and enforce."

---Stephen Elias
Bias Against the Pro Per
With Permission
Nolo Press

Preface

In the preceding foreword, Stephen Elias points to the prejudice that prevents the self-represented from having their "day" in court. The "pro per" must stand alone against the legal establishment. In cases involving fundamental rights he usually finds he is in a class targeted for discrimination by the same courts that deny the class exists. These participants in America's legal system, frequently the purveyors of truth, are victimized by a faulty system of law where equality is subject to judicial predicament.

Judicial impropriety is no stranger to members of the bar. Some attorneys benefit and even curry favor from corrupt courts. In these cases due process is often denied because or in spite of the assistance of counsel.

Attorneys of lesser power should be concerned. Theirs it seems is a position similar to the *pro se*. Should they resist, the court may reject their pleas and even subject them to loss of license.

Writing of the appearances of impropriety in an article in the Las Vegas Review Journal January 26, 2006, Associated Press writer Gina Holland tells of a plan by members of Congress that would require judges to make public the companies in which they have a financial interest and potential conflict. The plan may not go far enough. In 2002, twenty-two federal judges failed to report trips underwritten by major corporations, according to the article.

Conflicts for judges do not end with major corporations. Without adherence to existing law the guarantee of a fair trial is lost in a system of cronyism and judicial immunity.

Disgruntled judges that refuse to read the pleadings of the self-represented deny meaningful access to the courts.

A judge's bias, any form of it, destroys the integrity of that court.

The mere appearance of impropriety is reason for disqualification of a judge. Still, prejudice against the *pro per* is spread by the "idiot for attorney, fool for client" chicanery.

Meantime, the number of cases involving at least one self-represented party is growing. According to information released in the U.S. Ninth Circuit the number had swollen from 3,607 in the year 2000 to roughly over 5,000 in 2003. The percentage of cases in the 4th Circuit is higher, topping 50% *pro se*. There the circuit court makes extensive use of law students to assist the *pro se*, even to argue cases before it.

Nationally, the number of cases with a *pro se* party is near 50 percent. Recently, the Ninth Circuit declared its 39% figure a "logjam" and assigned a task force to make recommendations. Those recommendations may not be fully implemented. A visit to the Ninth's website and review of the *pro se* "package" of information and forms reveals neither policy shift nor significant change.

The *pro per* may find the same conditions in

appellate courts that he flees in the lower court, subjected again to lengthy delay and professional indifference.

Settled law preserves the right to self-counsel. But, in a counterfeit court, inherent rights are meaningless. As legal costs rise and corruption spreads more will suffer.

The author's experience is up close and personal. Immune System, In Search Of A Court of Law, reaches beyond our beliefs. One case representative of many, one litigant that could have been anyone, one right we take for granted, testing the standards of judicial conduct.

The forces that drive America's legal system it seems, are power, money, incompetence—or justice. There is ample evidence that justice is incompatible with the other three. The judicial system, self-immunized and self-perpetuating, offers no stamp of approval, no guarantee—even where due process is a core issue.

There is no national protection act for litigants. Once exposed to corruption, the would-be "whistle blower" is isolated against the system.

Is there corruption beyond belief?

There are numerous stories. This is one that made the victim the writer.

Introduction

Although issues remain, most of the litigation is over. I am, you might say, persona non grata in America's legal system. I have been barred, as in denied; blocked; shut-out, from defending myself against fraud in an Arizona superior court. Judgment was imposed even though the judge would not accept my pleadings, in defense of fraudulent claims.

But, I have not been denied the right to prosecute just claims in federal court—at least not yet.

Before being barred from Arizona's court I was unprofessionally represented by an incompetent attorney licensed by the State Bar of Arizona as a Specialist in Real Estate Law. To my knowledge Raymond Brown retains that distinction, even though the same state bar has since found him in breach of professional duty.

My appeal, pending in the Ninth Circuit, presents claims once found meritorious by order of a U.S. District judge. The claims established under applicable law, with evidence, may be proven beyond reasonable doubt--a standard higher than necessary. Regardless, the courts may not concede my victory because I am *pro se*.

I know that many of our citizens avoid court, some with good reason. Others out of fear of a broken system. In my case the courts have found reason to hide from me. It seems their mistakes should remain obscure.

The last U.S. District Judge, deciding matters, was represented in personal investments by the same law firm that represented my opponent, The Carioca Company, before him. A defendant in federal court, Carioca was the originator of the litigation in state court.

Should the federal judge have recused himself over a conflict of interest, or the appearance of impropriety? Did the courts of Arizona, federal and state, perpetrate a scam? Were the attorneys that represented me before I turned *pro se* negligent, and my opponent and its counsel in abuse of the legal process? I plan to answer those questions in the pages that follow.

Attorneys will tell you that judges are only human and that parties appearing before them must be careful not to rankle the robed resident of the bench. Could U.S. District Judge Robert C. Broomfield rise above his earthly constraints?

The self-represented often has only one weapon against the powerful: truth. But in a crooked court, the truth can be turned away and hidden by repeated abuse of the law of discovery and disclosure.

In the hands of a judge motivated by prejudice the system is turned upside down. And the system that was abused becomes the tool used to obstruct the due course of justice.

Respectable newspapers remind us daily of official neglect, corruption, and damage done by bad judges. Our system of government must rely upon a competent and honest judiciary. Yet lifetime federal appointments to the bench are influenced more by politics than judicial ability. State judges typically owe their positions to campaign managers and financial contributors instead of legal science or knowledge of law.

The judicial/prosecutorial side of law, whether civil or criminal, should have the same goal. But, investigations are turning up victims, many framed and executed in the name of justice--for crimes they did not commit! DNA evidence is difficult to dispute.

Therefore, it is hard to believe that a legal system that has sent innocent people to death row and beyond, cares about the victims of legal abuse in a civil court?

Documentary evidence is the DNA of civil law. However, corrupt courts often ignore documentary evidence in favor of business as usual.

Would a merit system of pay induce better jurisprudence? If decisions were subjected to review by impartial and qualified jurists, and pay and benefits merit-based, would we have better courts? For that matter, lower insurance premiums? Are high powered, heavily financed campaigns for judgeships good for America? Or would we be better served if all judges were nominated by the chief executive from a pool of legislative nominations, alternating with the political parties? There is obvious dissatisfaction with the present status, even among sitting judges. Increasing the salaries of judges will not cure the problems?

To bring about the necessary change the public must be informed. More of us have to stand on the side of the oppressed—those who are morally correct.

There can be little doubt that in our legal system absolute power corrupts. It is that power held by attorneys (I hesitate to call them lawyers because I believe that indicates a higher standard) and judges that obstructs legal process and devalues America. The message is: our system needs reform.

I never planned to be a messenger.

Power in the wrong hands is an awesome destructive force. The law provides that each of us should have a reasonable understanding of the law, an ability to know right from wrong, applicable as well to judges. Ignorance may not excuse us. I had my day in court. The law did not. The documentary evidence is in the record.

The story has just one beginning. Duty beckons.

Judge Edith Jones, United States Fifth Circuit Court, told the Federalist Society of Harvard Law School in 2003 that the American Legal System has been corrupted almost beyond recognition.

Article by Geraldine Hawkins,
March 7, 2003
MassNews.com

PART 1:

Times of Trial

The Specialist

I had made the early morning trek over Mingus Mountain many times. But this day was to be different. There was no job involved. I was not going bird hunting. The Carioca trial was coming to an end. It was Tuesday, March 18, 1997. We would hear the closing arguments and the instructions for jury deliberation.

On the way to Prescott, Bea made a list of the plaintiff's missing performances under a real estate contract. I shared thoughts on a substantial performance instruction the superior court judge planned to give the jury. In Court, our paralegal highlighted our list in red, then passed it to her husband, Raymond Brown. There was no comment from Ray. Soon the paper was buried with other notes and documents.

Raymond Brown, an Arizona State Bar certified Real Estate Specialist, had called me at home the night before to tell me the judge was not going to give any of his proposed instructions. Brown had rarely called, and never at night. He said he was upset, particularly about losing three instructions that dealt with forfeiture and strict performance of contracts. He explained how he felt betrayed by the judge. He said he would get over it, and have another chance in chambers the next morning.

Ray Brown had submitted a trial memorandum to the court in Judge Weaver's chambers at about 4:30 p.m., Monday. The memorandum was in support of his proposed jury instructions. Counsel made arguments and objections. Under some pressure, Brown apparently volunteered to remove some of the instructions in favor of others. His concessions did not help. Closing arguments were scheduled the next day.

In Arizona, the state bar offers special status to attorneys. A specialist in an area of law is supposed to be an expert in his field. He could reasonably be expected to bring something to the court that is lawfully substantial or significant. It is understood that he should know the fundamental law of his chosen specialty, and if he tries cases in court, then it would also be reasonable to believe his knowledge would be effectively applied at trial.

Tuesday came with surprises. The first when Raymond Brown started his closing argument with an apology for mistakes. He did not make clear what he felt they were, but obviously he had some on his mind. Then, he told the jury that he did not know whether I had told the truth or not, but he believed I had.

Brown's capitulation was near complete when Judge Weaver told him he had five minutes left. Wondering as if he were lost, Raymond Brown asked, "Five Minutes? How can I spend my last five minutes"? The question appeared to be directed at no one other than himself. That and other answers never came to Ray. He was lost, and we were losing.

Weaver did not give any of Brown's instructions to the jury.

That afternoon Jodie, Ray's spouse and legal assistant, sprang her own surprise. After lunch, waiting for the jury verdict, Jodie told us that Ray stayed away from home the previous night coming in Tuesday morning just to freshen up before attending court.

The news seemed the grand finale to a day full of surprises. The information left an uneasy feeling.

Ray had told me long before trial that he was going to be aggressive. When questions arose and I inquired of Ray on pre-trial matters, he became defensive. In anticipation of the pending trial he wrote me January 21, 1997:

"If, after the trial is over with and you remain dissatisfied with me and choose to pursue all of the remaining questions that you feel you need and want answers to, I promise you that I will do whatever is necessary to get you what you want. I would assume that, in pursuing the answers to the remaining questions, you would want to bring suit against me or to file an ethical complaint against me with the Arizona State Bar. You and I are fully aware that those avenues are open to you if you choose to pursue them. I hope that will not be necessary, but I will cooperate with you even under those circumstances."

After trial, I wrote Ray Brown advising him of my disappointment, thoughts and feelings. I said I felt he still intended to make good on his word. Ray wrote back saying he was insulted and going to quit. At the time Raymond Brown was on the board of governors of The Arizona State Bar. I heard he was in line to become its next president.

It doesn't matter much where Ray Brown spends

his last five minutes. It's his time thereafter that may be in jeopardy.

I don't think Brown ever became president of the bar. Although qualified he was instead found in breach of professional duties.

The essence of contract law is that one party may not demand performance of the other unless he himself has fully performed. Ordinarily, goods must be delivered before the buyer's duty to pay is due. The Carioca Company had not performed its obligations under a real estate contract, not even substantially. Documents settling the escrow and transferring the property had not been accurately prepared by Transamerica Title Company.

Transamerica is another book. Needless to say I have avoided Transamerica Title in subsequent dealings when the opportunity presented itself.

I had bought other real estate and believed that payment would be due when the escrow was correct and ready to close.

Ray Brown did not prove himself a specialist? A Prescott attorney that declined the case because as he said, he "refused to practice in Raymond Weaver's Court" recommended Brown to me. But, Brown proved undeserving of the trust. He was neither prepared nor effective at trial. Ray did not command the respect of his peer rivals.

We were left in a legal twilight zone. Attorneys in breach of ethics and duty. Judge Raymond Weaver outside the law, and biased.

But Weaver knew he was safe with Brown. He knew long before we did, I think, that Brown was non-adversarial. Weaver may have also known the law. The jury did not. They were caught between the scam and the scum. With a little help from his friend it became Weaver's web.

A court of law is more than a judge. A court is made up of the players and parties necessary to conduct the business of a court. Attorneys of record, the judge, the clerk, and the litigants comprise the court. In the case at hand the opposing attorney, found Brown inadequate, seized the opportunity and misused the legal process. The record indicates Judge Weaver was often entertained by antic rather than compelled by law. It was the classic kangaroo court, in a civil setting.

From the other side of misuse of process and legal negligence, I became sort of a specialist. I learned that Rules are subject to change in a counterfeit court. Incompetence can obliterate the prospect of equal treatment under law.

Ray Brown, it seems, could get over Weaver's betrayal—even survive incompetence. He would still demand his fee and continue his practice. I was to take the blow, as do others who are ill served. Those we must trust do not always hold the law in high regard. My education was to be continued.

Miraculous Appearances

Through the best part of four days in March 1997, in the old high ceilinged courthouse of Prescott, Arizona's mile high city, we went to court with Carioca. Roughrider Bucky O'Neil symbolic of America's past and his mount in bronze just outside. We waited and remembered the dream; that every American can have his day before a competent judge, a jury of peers, with a champion of the law to tell his story.

Carioca had sued for "Declaratory Judgment" and in their complaint alleged that I had acted in bad faith and breached a real estate contract. Discovery incomplete, the truth would be avoided by our negligent attorney, Raymond Brown.

The original set of trial exhibits lost for a week, reappeared just before trial. When confronted with a duplicate set of exhibits, appearing under unusual circumstance, Judge Raymond Weaver credited Carioca's counsel Albert Van Wagner for his clairvoyance. Weaver said he didn't know what happened to the originals.

The originals, however, re-surfaced in the clerk's office. In chambers, the record shows, the clerk asked "What do you want me to do with those?"

Weaver replied, "The new ones?"

"The ones that miraculously appeared", the clerk answered.

Van Wagner's flippant comment, apparently entertaining to Judge Weaver was, "Hillary must have been here." Hillary, Clinton that is, was then the First Lady. On the national scene the Whitewater Investigation had been going for some time. Missing records needed in the far-flung Arkansas scandal were eventually found in a closet of the White House. The event triggered more suspicions and allegations.

Closer to home the clerk reached a sinister conclusion, saying that the exhibits were only the plaintiff's. Caution was thrown to the wind.

Some documents, I later discovered, were either altered or mismatched with other critical items of evidence. The survey plat of the property done in January 1994 became falsified evidence. Carioca added a date to the plat to make it look like the survey was made in December 1994. A comparison of the blue print made from the sepia in January with the blue print offered in evidence reveals that a handwritten date was added--the only difference in the two plat maps.

The map, actually made in January 1994 while Carioca was claiming good faith in our deal, was in truth made for one Leonard J. Steele, taking title eventually as Verde Hospitality, LLC.

My attorney Raymond Brown did not make a proper challenge to the miracles that appeared in Weaver's court.

A Prescott attorney told me later that if

confronted with his negligence Raymond Brown would probably say he "played cards with Jesus Christ."

Regardless, on the first ballot the jury voted 6 to 3 in my favor. On a subsequent vote the jury favored Carioca 8 to 1. After the judgment, I sent a survey to the jurors. Five of the nine responded some telling me that I did not have a good attorney. One of the jurors wrote on a post-trial survey, "I don't think you were represented very well at all."

Dereliction of duty and misuse of process may skirt the boundary of criminal intent. Incompetence, however, is not a crime. The juror was right about Brown's representation, but the jury was wrong in their verdict. They were denied crucial evidence and testimony, and given bad instruction.

I hold no animas with the jury. They probably did their best under the circumstance.

After a failed appeal, other attorneys told me to give up--the deck is stacked! So? Are we a nation of laws? I was determined to pursue an answer. If the deck was stacked what happened to law? Did we degrade ourselves to a third world system of cronyism and recompense? Would the misuse of process that started in state court continue, even in federal court? Since I was then a resident of Nevada, would the federal courts hear my state claims of malpractice and abuse of process, under diversity of citizenship?

For the many years that followed, higher courts yielded to the corruption of an inferior state court and turned away the precept of equal justice under law. Eventually the Bar's legal counsel would advise staff to have no further contact with me. Meanwhile a state judge would recuse himself, another would be disqualified; an insurer providing malpractice coverage would belly up and Raymond Brown's carrier would sever its ties with him.

The Value of Misinformation

In 1993, I placed $40,000.00 in escrow with Transamerica Title Company as a deposit to purchase vacant land near I-17 and highway 260 in Camp Verde, Arizona. The escrow was scheduled to close December 31, 1993. For various reasons, most unknown to me at the time, instruments of escrow were not available for closing. Those that were available contained error. The only thing preventing the closing, as far as I knew then, was my unwillingness to have the escrow close with errors. Otherwise, I was ready, willing, and able to close.

Requests for correction were made through Transamerica Title Company, and the seller's broker/agent Jack Bird. Continuing negotiations over easements, signage, and access slowed and came to a stop in January. Still, believing that the escrow would close soon, I placed more money from an exchange into the escrowed trust account with Transamerica Title Company.

Then, I began receiving letters from an attorney, threatening suit on behalf of Carioca. I answered each letter and sought correction and explanation.

Carioca's letter canceling escrow came in late

January 1994. Carioca, the seller, maintained it had performed. In its notice Carioca made demand for the earnest money. With my response and objection Transamerica held all funds pending a civil action to decide the matter. Two months later Carioca filed suit.

Into February, I had stood ready to close the escrow with Carioca. Then it became clear that Carioca would not perform, was demanding that I perform first, and planning to sue me.

Years after I would learn that The Carioca Company made arrangements to sell the property to another buyer, while pretending it wanted to close the deal with me. To seal its other deal Carioca entered into a dubious Real Estate Listing with Montezuma Land Co., through its Broker Jack P. Bird. Dick Pogue's name was shown as the Listing agent. Phony on its face the Listing was created in bad faith. It would prove to be the subject of volumes of legal pleadings and court orders.

In state court, my attorney Raymond Brown disclosed the Listing as Defendant's Exhibit 103. But Brown never possessed the original. Ray had received a copy of the Listing, apparently in files from Carioca's attorney. Ray did not do discovery on the Listing. Disclosing and filing exhibits without knowing the facts would seem to be a cardinal sin in legal practice.

Brown did not know the relevant facts.

Thanks to Brown's negligence we knew little about Carioca's undisclosed deal. The document Brown entered into evidence had not been examined under discovery. The Listing was presumed to have been created January 3, 1993.

However, records obtained years later from the Arizona Department of Real Estate showed that Richard "Dick" Pogue was not licensed with Montezuma in January 1993.

Following a hunch, I had decided to clear up issues with the Listing. Why was Pogue the "Listing agent"? How long had he worked for Jack Bird's Montezuma Realty? I contacted the Arizona Department of Real Estate in March, 2002. From email exchanges with Cindy Ferrin, Director of Customer Relations, I learned that Richard Pogue, indeed, was not licensed with Montezuma Realty in January 1993.

I thought I needed a certified copy of Pogue's license, for federal court. It would take a week or more to receive the license history from the ADRE, and then I would be subject to possible problems with the mail. So, I contacted a private investigator, Rich Coppinger, in the Phoenix area.

Coppinger, R.C. Investigations, was able to get a certified copy and send it to me. For the money I paid Rich it was well worth not having to drive some 800 miles round trip, or face a delay.

My negotiations with Carioca had begun in September 1993. The Listing surfaced in litigation, in 1996. The truth about the Listing was a result of my informal discovery made in 2002. The Listing is evidence, a direct link to Carioca's misuse of the legal process, and Raymond Brown's neglect.

Carioca's intent with its Listing became more obvious. It was covering a base with Jack Bird, while moving to replace its deal with me.

In post-judgment hearings Carioca's President Marvin Rose and Bird admitted they prepared the

Listing. It is not entirely clear why they printed Pogue's name on the Listing. Rose testified that Pogue was a friend. Pogue, it appears, was then a resident of Missouri. He was probably considered an unlikely prospect for testimony in Arizona, even if the truth were to be uncovered.

Brown's attorneys in federal court, defending him in the malpractice suit, quit him probably because of his mishandling of evidence in state court. His counsel wrote in one of their late pleadings that it believed much would be said in federal court about the agreement, referring of course to the fraudulent Listing of Carioca and its agent Montezuma Land Co.

Carioca's broker had a duty to retain the Listing for a period of five years, according to state law. After the litigation began in 1994, all parties would have the obligation under law to preserve it as evidence and make a proper disclosure to the court. Regardless, the original of the Listing was lost; or destroyed perhaps, by Carioca's agents or officers.

My motions to determine fact based upon the evidence were denied by Senior District Judge Robert C. Broomfield. Broomfield claimed he did not see the connection. Later, and to my surprise I found the connection ran deeper than I thought. Meanwhile though, the examination of the evidence that I requested in federal court was not available.

There was still, that public record of the Listing created by Brown's incomplete disclosure in state court.

Carioca and Montezuma did not create the phony Listing for fun. Plainly, they did not plan to make an honest disclosure. They were motivated to confuse their opposition and to conceal their other deal. If the Listing was created in 1994, as the evidence indicates, then the Listing was made in rejection of Carioca's contract and escrow with me; evidence of repudiation that Carioca could ill afford.

The Listing between Carioca and Bird cuts like a two edged sword. On the one hand it points directly at Carioca's ultimate use of legal process to achieve an ulterior purpose. On the other, it shows Raymond Brown's legal negligence in failing to do discovery of the evidence he disclosed.

Bird would lie in a post-judgment hearing in state court claiming that I called him from Nevada, with word that I had changed my mind about going through with the Carioca escrow. Judge Lindberg, standing and on his way out of the courtroom, permitted Bird to make his statement after the hearing in 2002 had ended. It may not be on the record.

Bird's tale was constructed to help Carioca. Bird wanted the court to believe that I had waived some condition in 1994. He thought his lie was supported in part by fact.

Bird knew that I owned a house in Henderson, Nevada, but apparently did not know when I bought it. The house was built and purchased in 1996. Bird had claimed that I called him from Henderson, while the escrow with Carioca was pending. That might have been believable, if I had lived there in 1994. Carioca filed its suit in March that year.

Bird was not one to let the facts get in his way.

Jack Bird had honed his skills in scrapes with authorities in Flagstaff and Camp Verde, Arizona--

over many years. Leland McPherson, city manager of Flagstaff when I served on the council there, often said you can't win a pissing contest with a skunk. Many times it was said in regard of Jack Bird.

As they say, a bell cannot be unrung. Although state replacement Judge Thomas Lindberg had found the evidence of fraud troubling and of interest he took no action. In contrast federal judge Broomfield found the matter of no significance. Their flawed analysis is better understood now.

In federal court, Brown admitted he never knew the Listing's date, but in his motion for summary judgment argued it wasn't 1994. Given a choice of either '93 or '94, and not knowing which, Brown's argument against either year was ill motivated.

Brown's irrational argument should have been enough to cause Broomfield to scrutinize the evidence and consider Brown's motive.

To cover his negligence in the state litigation, the malpractice claim squarely in front of U. S. District Judge Broomfield, Brown argued that a 1994 Listing did not exist. Brown was left with a strange paradox—a public record--a real estate Listing that he disclosed that he could not date. One he failed to subject to discovery, but would argue was not created in the only year the evidence can support. All the while admitting that he never possessed the original and did not know the year the Listing was made.

Although the year was yet to be decided in court, a fact material and genuine, substance for appeal was found in Brown's admission of his neglect.

In full view of Brown's conflict co-defendant Albert E. Van Wagner, Jr., Carioca's former attorney, asserted conflicting purposes for the Listing. In state court Van Wagner explicitly declared the "Listing was made for the Verde Sale." Verde, aka Verde Hospitality LLC, did not exist in 1993. Verde was created by Leonard Steele and his partners in September 1994.

Van Wagner's statement was significant.

In federal court and in conflict, Van Wagner contradicted himself asserting the Listing had nothing to do with the Verde sale. Van Wagner's statements either deceived the courts or helped set their role of misconduct in a scheme of fraud and deception.

Carioca took a less assertive position alleging it "appeared" its Listing's date was 1993. Since it was their Listing and their President signed it, you would expect them to know. But a weak and uncertain response from crooks held the day in federal court.

Misinformation would prove invaluable to the defendants in Broomfield's court. Misinforming the court in association with the other defendants became a defense strategy.

Broomfield and the defendants ignored the fact that Pogue was not licensed in 1993. Their disregard of material evidence was deliberate. Brown, it seemed, had breached his duty by not examining the document to learn the material facts. It was not his only breach.

Unfortunately incompetence and corruption in our courts has a price—more staff, more space, more time. An overburdened public pays for the waste. And the injustice threatens all people everywhere.

Bias Permitted

Federal law dictates that issues of fact must be determined by the fact finder. In an order filed May 12, 2003 Judge Broomfield deferred fact finding to the trial. A jury demand had been made; the jury would be the decider of fact. Judge Broomfield was the trier of law.

The defendants' failure to disclose true and complete information about their real estate Listing appeared deliberate. It conveyed false and misleading impressions. There was, it seemed, more unknown than known about Carioca's late breaking agreement.

After my motion to determine fact was denied by Judge Broomfield, each defendant filed a motion for summary judgment. If a summary motion were denied, the case or some part of it, would move forward on the merits. If the motions were granted, then the case would end with summary judgment in defendants' favor. Brown, Van Wagner, and Carioca were trying to avoid a jury trial.

Settled law provides the procedure the court was to follow in reaching its summary judgment decision. The primary duty of the judge is to decide if there are genuine issues of dispute that would influence the fact finder's decision. In a toss up the benefit of doubt goes to the non-mover.

Questions and disputes arose over matters of discovery, concealment, intent, motive, and good faith--all issues of fact. Broomfield was not supposed to determine fact, infer fact, or weigh the issues. He was obligated to view the evidence in a light favorable to me. I was the non-movant. The defendants, movers under the motion, had the duty to demonstrate a lack of genuine dispute in the case.

Written argument was made for and against summary disposition. After the court was briefed, Broomfield granted summary judgment in favor of the defendants. There is no way to know whether he or a clerk read the briefs. But, his orders leading to judgment were replete with error.

On motion, an amended Judgment was entered July 14, 2004. An appeal to the Ninth Circuit was docketed July 27, 2004. The last brief under appeal was filed January 3, 2005. The appeal is still pending.

Whether Broomfield's errors will be noted and properly dealt with on appeal remains to be seen. Regardless of the outcome the errors are plain for all to see.

The summary judgment decision was based in deception and false inferences. In the claim of legal malpractice the evidence of record under applicable state law prohibited Broomfield from granting summary judgment. Brown's neglect had been decided! His duty and relationship were admitted! Of the elements of malpractice, causation and damages required finding of fact, a jury's decision.

The case against Brown clearly was not suited for summary judgment! Because genuine issues were in dispute with Brown, summary judgment could not be lawfully granted.

In the Arizona case of *Collins v. Miller & Miller* the Arizona Supreme Court ruled that a plaintiff (that's me in federal court) must prove he would have been successful in the prior case, but for his attorney's negligence. The standard of proof is a fact finder's standard. Broomfield was not the fact finder in the case before him (CV 00 0497 PCT RCB). The jury demand precluded him from making a determination of fact (proof).

By granting summary judgment, Broomfield erred on the side of the movant Raymond Brown.

Clearly Broomfield made error of law. The decision should be overturned on appeal.

Similarly, in the abuse of process claim, Judge Broomfield made material error of law in deciding that instances of misuse of process in his court could not be brought before him.

Broomfield was obligated to follow state law in the diversity proceeding. Would a federal judge disregard his duty under law?

It is necessary to look beyond the record. Motive has to be examined. Innuendo, false statement, and half-truth were used liberally by the defendants in their motions and replies for summary judgment.

Genuine disputes remain with Carioca and Van Wagner over good faith, even the worthiness of its state suit. Issues in dispute, even those not in contention in state court were subject to examination in the abuse of process claim in federal court. Some were at the core of the case before Broomfield, but evidently he did not want to go there.

Reason can tell us that the co-defendants had a common goal, to terminate the litigation. This mutually motivated triad had motive to lie, if necessary. And to bypass the evidence, it became necessary. In acts of deception the associated defendants put forward irrational argument contrary to the evidence. In simple analysis the defendants abused the legal process more; protecting themselves by lying, each for the other.

At least one defendant was represented by a law firm that was also representing Judge Broomfield in his Bell Grande investments, in Phoenix.

An organization with a web presence at www.judicialwatch.org made known the financial disclosures of federal judges in early 2005. As I write, the information is still available on the Judicial Watch website, but only for 2003. It was however, that year's disclosure that captured my interest. Why there has been no disclosure for 2004 or 2005 remains a question.

Reasonable minds may agree that the Listing was made in 1994 for Carioca's negotiations with Leonard J. Steele. Steele was the prime mover in the creation of Verde Hospitality, LLC, the buyer of record in 1994. Furthermore, it is unlikely the term of the Listing was three years. The image of the Listing follows page after next. It is presented just as it was filed with the court.

Given the chance, a jury could determine material fact, including the date of the Listing's creation. In addition to the matter of Pogue's not being licensed, there is other fact that would help the jury decide when the Listing was created.

Notably, our escrow agreement, signed in October 1993, made no mention of a Real Estate Listing.

Raymond Brown neglected his duty by failing to discover that Pogue was not licensed with Bird (Montezuma) in January 1993. Carioca failed to address and correct the misinformation that was conveyed with Brown's incomplete disclosure. The evidence indicates the Listing was fraudulently created, and defendants' falsehoods crafted to deceive the courts.

Forensic tests made from a copy of a written instrument would be of little, if any, help. Regardless, and in spite of Carioca destroying or losing the original Listing, all known evidence about the Listing indicates that it was created on or about January 3, 1994.

Some of the defendants some of the time have alleged the Listing was made in 1993. It is possible though unlikely that the Carioca agent dated the Listing with a January 1993 date inadvertently. Many of us make error in dates that are so close to the start of a new year. But an innocent mistake would not change the materiality of a Listing actually made in 1994, and dated as 1993.

Carioca did not act in good faith. Carioca had proven itself a trickster. Its Listing was in anticipation of canceling its deal. It was an act of repudiation. Carioca's litigation was an abuse of the legal process.

The court was informed of its misinformation,

and its bias in favor of the defendants. Broomfield's decision would become final if not overturned on appeal, and would preclude jury fact-finding. Federal Senior Judge Broomfield would have unlawfully assumed the role of jury.

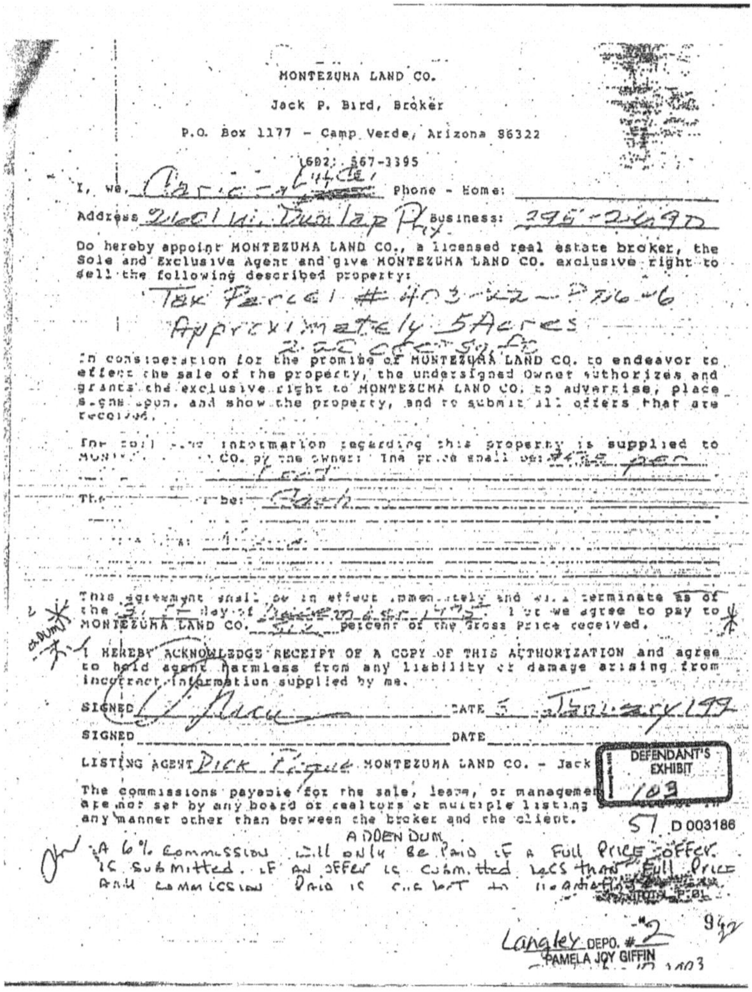

Image 1
The unabridged document recorded in Yavapai
Superior Court Cause CV 94-0249 as Defendants'
Exhibit 103

Immune System

The Substantial Standard

In state court Judge Raymond Weaver seemed to believe that Carioca had somehow met a substantial performance standard. In Weaver's world the seller would be allowed to partially perform its obligations, while the buyer would be held to specific performance of the contract terms.

It is difficult if not impossible to find a place for substantial performance in a real estate deal. In analogy, would the buyer pay the full price if he didn't get all the property? An Arizona appeals judge said he had trouble with that possibility. But not enough, it seems, to bother the judge's conscience or cause correction.

The list of factual statements, shown on the next page, did not come from thin air. The list is posted on the Internet at www.leafmark.com. An attorney, reading it for the first time on the Internet, sent me an email saying "I love your piece on 'you had a fair trial, if.' It's a work of art!" The ten statements are based upon fact.

Weaver misapplied the law. Substantial performance of contract terms carries with it certain legal conditions. The party that does not fully perform must be of good faith, willing and able to complete its obligations. These conditions required fact finding by the jury. However, there was no fact finding in the Weaver Court. The jury issued a general verdict without deciding whether Carioca was willing and able to close.

The jury did not make an express finding of either good or bad faith.

The jury was evidently unaware that Carioca had failed to meet the conditions of substantial performance.

Carioca demonstrated its repudiation of the deal. Some of the evidence is in the record of the state trial. Evidence is also found in the disclosures and discovery in federal court. Included are Carioca's refusal to present and sign the escrow documents of transfer and closure—evidence of Carioca's unwillingness to perform. Further, if not conclusively, Carioca negotiated agreements with its agents, and third parties that led to its sale to Verde.

Evidence of Carioca's bad faith is demonstrated in the falsified Listing agreement, its survey of the property for another, and in its specific agreements with others for an entry sign and access.

In acts and with intent Carioca repudiated our real estate agreement.

Without objection from our attorney, Judge Weaver presented the jury the wrong view of simple contract law. Fundamental concepts and doctrine including the statute of frauds, specific performance, and equal treatment in the standards of performance were overlooked.

You Had A Fair Trial in Arizona, If:

(Laughable, but non-fiction!)

1. The trial exhibits were lost for a week, but only a few key documents were tampered with.

2. You were extorted, but the Court didn't make you do jail time.

3. The judge said substantial performance was good enough in a real estate contract, but asked, "Do we reward stupidity?"

4. Your attorney, a "Certified Real Estate Specialist," repeatedly calls a draft of a legal description a deed, and an unrecordable, unsigned and undated document an easement.

5. The county attorney tells you to ". . .not only, refer the case to the State Bar for disciplinary action, but to also file a motion in the original trial court to set aside the judgment."

6. Your former attorney prints your legal abuse website and sends it to the State Bar claiming you are "out of control."

7. You claim perjury, and a key witness against you claims "absolute privilege," "Judicial Immunity," and "freedom from the fear that their actions in that position might adversely effect [sic] their personal interest."

8. Your appeals attorney says he's sorry the system failed, but you should get over it.

9. The Real Estate Broker never testifies at trial, and your attorney tells you he "forgot" to call him.

10. A big legal beagle turns his back on fraud and corruption, but "wishes you well."

Image 2

A page from http://www.leafmark.com, formerly at updoc.com

Appeals Attorney Donald Peters said Ray Brown didn't object to Carioca's "substantial-compliance" instruction. Brown's neglect caused damage. Brown did not protect or preserve a critical defense issue. He failed to object to the standard of substantial performance by the seller, Carioca.

Discovery should have revealed the last essential facts. But Brown's discovery was incomplete. Jack Bird, Carioca's broker/agent could have given key testimony at trial about the phony Listing and unprepared easements, if Brown had called him to testify.

Judge Weaver struck the fatal blow when he gave the jury his "substantial performance" instruction. It seems obvious that the standard of substantial cannot reasonably coexist with a conflicting standard of strict performance. Perhaps unduly influenced, or lacking independent knowledge, Judge Weaver made the final error in the state trial.

In federal court, Carioca would lower the bar even further claiming that it either performed its duty under agreement or it was "excused" from performance. Carioca offered no evidence of its alleged performance, and it did not attempt to explain who would have excused it from performance of agreement in 1993-94.

Of course, no one excused Carioca. Crooks though do not need excuse, merely opportunity.

Could due process or equal protection under law be so easily denied? If so, then the equal treatment under law guarantee was a stranger to the state courts.

The Brotherhood

A judge doing his duty of finding law, and fact where applicable, may require attorneys to bring relevant cases to his court. Lawful instructions to a jury are dependent upon the judge's integrity and this process. Did Judge Raymond Weaver know the law? Did he act on knowledge of law or was he personally influenced?

It would be nice to know what is in a man's soul, but our law does not require that.

Federal rights are inherently a part of any process in a court of law. Federal question issues presented here are plainly in the complaint and pleadings in federal court. On its face the record demonstrates the claim of right to equal treatment. Due process and equal treatment are not trumped by other doctrine of law or constitutional provision.

Lindberg, the last state judge to have contact with the case, held that claims of fraud upon the court are subject to expire under Rule 60 of the Civil Rules of Arizona. However the U.S. 7th Circuit Court of Appeals said, "We think, however, that it can be reasoned that a decision produced by fraud on the court is not in essence a decision at all, and never becomes final." *Drobny v. C.I.R.*, (7th Cir., 1997) No. 95-2966.

"Fraud upon the court" has been defined by the 7th Circuit Court to "embrace that species of fraud which does, or attempts to, defile the court itself, or is a fraud perpetrated by officers of the court so that the judicial machinery can not perform in the usual manner its impartial task of adjudging cases that are presented for adjucation."

For further reference see, *Kenner v. CI.R.* 387 F 2d 689 (7th Cir.), cert. denied, 393 U.S. 841 (1968); and, Moore's Federal Practice, 2d ed., p 512, 60. 23.

It may appear to the non-believer that the courts in this case would rather err on the side of attorneys than to be right on the side of the *pro per.* Unchecked, the practice of cronyism in the courts turns the nation away from law. Understanding this judicial condition can aid the victim in the search for justice.

Courts are not allowed to place conditions on the vindication of a federal right; e.g. the right to a fair trial. So far in this case, the courts have merely ignored the matter. Therefore the issue of equal treatment in the standards of contract performance have not been litigated. The matter apparently remains; live and unadjudicated.

The attorneys and judges that came in contact with these issues may not have attended the "school of justice," or any top rated law school. How likely is it, though, that their common goal was to deny and suppress unwelcome claims?

At a recess in the state trial Raymond Brown

told me he thought we would win the case. He said he didn't see how we could lose. The evidence, he felt, was compelling and testimony was in our favor. I agree, the case could have been won on the merits.

We eventually learned that Raymond Brown failed to mount the most obvious defenses. An appeal to a higher state court would not reverse the damage.

In defense of his own role in the state appeal, attorney Donald Peters alleged that some of our issues could not be presented because of Brown's failure to preserve them at trial. According to Peters, the real issues were not even presented under appeal. The memorandum opinion seems to confirm his belief. In that shortcoming, I believe Don Peters bought a share.

Were there issues that might have been, or should have been presented on appeal? Did Peters avoid issues that were politically embarrassing and patently obvious? Did he concede false fact or error of law? There is no doubt that fault lies with Raymond Brown. Brown has blamed others, but I don't believe he alleged the fault of Peters.

Brown, at the time, was a member of the Board of Governors of The State Bar of Arizona. It is troubling, that during the course of the appeal Peters himself became protective of Brown. But before he did, Peters wrote saying that Carioca's attorney (Van Wagner) "thought Ray was 'in the bottom five percent' of all lawyers he had seen try cases." He said that Van Wagner might be a witness in a malpractice suit against Brown. As naïve as we may have been, I found that unlikely, even at the time. I could not imagine Van Wagner doing anything that might expose fraud, misuse of process, or jeopardize his client's victory.

Time does not permit the full examination of relationships and roles impacted by the Bar's brotherhood. That story will have to be done by others, It's ages old and it continues today.

The jurors, not allowed to hear crucial evidence and wrongfully instructed, were also denied access to the law. Prior to appeal in state court Don Peters wrote, "All parties will be better off if the errors of law in this case are acknowledged now rather than after a lengthy appeal."

Weaver denied our motion for a new trial, or to alter or amend judgment. There was no indication that Weaver read Peters' pleading.

Even Ray Brown had complained that Weaver did not read his memorandum on the proposed jury instructions. But he failed to make objection, or to preserve the issue. Meanwhile, Weaver was evidently comfortable with his mistakes.

In minute entries and orders, Weaver often seemed disoriented. He referred to the "absence of the Plaintiff's acceptance of the second deed." Before him, I was the defendant. Any deed submitted would have been by Carioca, the seller. Arguably they would have accepted the deed if they presented it.

In spite of Weaver's confused state, a correct deed did not exist.

Responding to my letter of inquiry, Judge Weaver wrote a brief reply. In two sentences he said it was "not appropriate for him to respond." Errors of fact and law overtopping reasoned complaint or inquiries are effective ways of obstructing justice. Weaver apparently did not want to face his mistakes.

Judge Weaver, in his role as trier of law, at numerous times, had been rendered incompetent.

In our judicial system accountability is hard to achieve.

On June 12, 2001, Judge Raymond Weaver resigned from the case and abandoned the bench in Yavapai Superior Court Cause CV 94-0249. Facing motions to compel disclosure and a motion for an impartial due process hearing, he simply recused himself, choosing to turn matters over to Judge Thomas Lindberg for all further proceedings.

Judge Weaver's acts were not designed to take a bite out of crime. He wanted another piece of me, to send the message again that in this case the truth was not welcome. Before leaving the bench Judge Weaver issued a minute entry in the court imposing sanctions upon me. The sanctions, $1000.00 in favor of Transamerica Title the original co-defendant in Carioca's fraudulent suit for declaratory judgment were nothing more than another abuse intended to penalize me for telling the truth.

With a high regard for fundamental rights, it seemed necessary that we continue the fight.

Retired Arizona Appeals Judge John Malloy author of The Fraternity: Lawyers and Judges in Collusion, Published by Paragon House said, "the once-honorable profession of law now fully functions as a bottom-line business, driven by greed and the pursuit of power and wealth."

John Malloy
In The Arizona Republic
March 27, 2005

PART 2:

The Federal Case

Immune System

Meritorious "State" Claims

The claims of legal malpractice and abuse of process were brought in federal court in March 2000, as CIV 00 0497 PCT. Random draw assigned the case to Senior U.S. District Judge Earl Carroll. Very early Judge Caroll recused himself, without making public his reason. The case was then reassigned to Senior U.S. District Judge Robert C. Broomfield.

I submitted a letter to the Circuit Executive's office requesting an interview with the chief judge. I wanted to learn more about the judge selection process. The letter was properly addressed. I felt the information requested was more generic than case specific.

The Circuit Executive's office informed me that the chief judge would not answer questions. Neither would she grant an interview.

It appeared to me that senior judges handled more a simple majority of cases involving a *pro per*. But senior judges do not make up a majority of the court. It seemed there was room for questions. Could the system of selecting a judge be rigged?

It would be a contribution to the public interest

if the record of cases filed by *pro pers* in the district court of Arizona were made available. Incidentally, there is only one case, I am aware of that survived a Broomfield dismissal. Judge Broomfield was overturned in *James v. Madison St Jail,* U.S. Ninth Circuit No. 9616384.

At the time of filing the action in 2000 I was a resident of Nevada, and had been since April 1996. All the defendants named in the federal suit were residents of Arizona. Therefore, I was entitled to bring legitimate claims in federal court, under diversity of citizenship. Diversity was established since all the defendants were residents of Arizona.

Early in our case and after a round of motions to dismiss, Judge Broomfield issued an order that would dispose of my suit; although he had previously found that my claims against Carioca's former counsel Van Wagner for abuse of process and Raymond Brown for malpractice were merited. In his order Judge Broomfield said the claims belonged in state court.

In a motion for reconsideration, I requested that the claims be reinstated and continued against Carioca, as well as Van Wagner and Brown. I asked that the case be continued in federal court under diversity. Of course, the defendants opposed the motion.

In his order that followed, Judge Broomfield found diversity of citizenship among the parties. He decided the federal case would continue against the three defendants.

Meritorious state claims in a federal court are to be treated essentially the same as if they were in state court. Under diversity the substantive law of

Arizona was to be applied. Federal statutory and settled law made the substantive law of Arizona controlling.

With few exceptions a federal court has its choice of state or federal rules. In most instances the rules are the same. However, there are some areas of law in which the state provides a different procedural rule. A choice of rules had little or no significance in federal court. What did matter was the use or, as it turned out, the misuse of the significant law of the case.

Closely related to malicious prosecution in criminal cases, abuse of process usually occurs where a party uses the legal machinery to achieve an illegitimate objective. Paragraph 682, the Restatement of Torts (Second), reads in part: "One who uses a legal process, whether criminal or civil, against another primarily to accomplish a purpose for which it is not designed, is subject to liability to the other for harm caused by the abuse of process."

Abuse and misuse, it seems, are not distinguishable in the tort. Pursuant to Arizona law the elements of abuse of process are: 1) an ulterior purpose, and 2) a willful act in the use of the process not proper in the regular conduct of the proceeding. Some definite act or threat not authorized by the process, or aimed at an objective not legitimate in the use of the process, may be required.

Litigation is a process that may be, and often is, misused. Taking someone to court under a false claim of bad faith and breach of contract appear to be a misuse of process. Likewise, taking someone to court in order to renege on a contract and to take or threaten to take an earnest deposit could provide the elements of the claim. False statement, bad faith disclosure, misrepresentation, concealment and distortion usually shape the evidence of the claim.

In Arizona claims of abuse of process may be brought in an existing case by amendment or motion. In the alternative the claim may be brought as an independent action, even after the process concludes. Time to bring the claim may be extended, tolled in other words, in some situations.

Once a court disposes of a case it is unusual for another court to examine claims of misconduct, regardless of relevance. Judicial protocol typically favors the prevailing party in all matters of appeal or review. It apparently does not matter whether the disfavored action was in state or federal court, or remanded (moved) from one to the other.

A judge may disfavor an abuse of process claim, especially it seems, if it was initiated by a *pro per*. In the instance of disposing of unwelcome claims a court can lose its integrity.

Notably, Arizona applies a liberal standard to abuse of process claims. A number of recent cases out of Division Two (Tucson) of the Arizona Appeals court have upheld the plaintiff's right to bring the claim. Those cases have plainly set legal precedent under Arizona law. My case in federal court, brought under diversity of citizenship, would test the integrity of the judge. Failing the test, would the appellate panel of judges in the Ninth Circuit reverse, and finally apply the law of the Forum State?

There are many federal judges of recent that have no experience in the state courts. They generally are selected from positions of a U.S. Attorney's office or some other federal service. In contrast however, there are many senior judges that served on a state bench before becoming a federal judge. Broomfield had been a state judge.

The surviving claims in Broomfield's court were state claims and could have been brought in state court. I had already been denied redress and correction in the Arizona courts. There appeared to be little chance that the courts of Arizona would be receptive to new claims, even if a federal court had found them meritorious.

In orders of late issue, Judge Broomfield declared that he would deny a motion to amend the complaint, if I brought it before him. His predetermination to deny just claims became an issue of error brought under appeal to the Ninth Circuit Court.

Immune System

Beyond A Doubt

The reader should be aware that I have presented a layman's view of the law. I have tried to minimize references to settled law, choosing not to present lengthy legal citations or quoted material. For further reading and a more in-depth study of the law applied, you may see the bibliography in the appendix. In most instances the referenced material is available on the Internet, including FindLaw, Cornell University, or GSU College of Law, Websites.

Judge Broomfield went wrong in deciding to dismiss the claims against the defendants at the summary judgment phase. Fundamentally, the law decided by the U.S. Supreme Court in *Anderson*, is that a trial court is precluded from fact finding in summary judgment decision. Beyond a doubt the district court failed to exercise reasonable decision making skills in denying discovery requests. Decisions were made based on clear error.

Broomfield knew that the element of causation in the malpractice claim against Brown was in dispute. He labored over the matter in his final orders. The genuine dispute is a matter of fact, that could only be decided by a jury in the case before him.

In the abuse of process claim Broomfield decided that my evidence must predate the filing of my claim in federal court. However, the law of Arizona established the right to bring claims of abuse of process in the case before him. The decisions of Arizona's appellate courts are reasonable and lawful.

It stands to reason that a party should not be allowed to continually and repetitiously abuse the legal process by simply continuing to give false testimony, deceive the court, or fail to make good faith disclosure. Broomfield knew that Carioca and Van Wagner could and likely would commit abuse of process in his court.

Broomfield's actions were to deny me access to the law of the forum state. In addition, he altered Arizona's liberal view of processes that may be abused. Finally, he denied me the freely given right of the Ninth Circuit to amend my pleading.

Far from law, Broomfield decided factual issues and dismissed material evidence. In matters of Caroca's intent and good faith Broomfield made false inferences. In the Listing disputes, property survey, an entry sign, the size of the parcel, as well as Carioca's claim of loss on its sale to Verde, Judge Broomfield made false determinations of fact.

Clearly, the decision for Judge Broomfield was whether there were any genuine issues of fact in dispute. If there were, then the court's duty was to move the issues to the fact-finding stage. There a jury would make the decisions.

To be genuine the issues must be material and

determinative; that is, capable of making a difference in the final outcome of the case.

To be fair and impartial Broomfield should have considered each issue to see if it was in dispute, without weighing evidence. A key question for Judge Broomfield was whether the finding of fact would have made a difference for either party. Some of the genuine issues of fact in dispute are:

- Whether the Carioca defendants acted in good faith in canceling its escrow agreement. (The question relates to discovery matters and Carioca's failure to perform. In making decisions, Judge Broomfield would be required by law to examine motive and intent.)
- Whether the defendants abused the legal process in federal court making incomplete and erroneous disclosures.
- Whether Carioca was excused from performance of contract as it claimed it was as seller in the real estate contract.
- Whether Carioca partially performed the terms of contract as seller. (And if it did was the standard of substantial performance adequate as a matter of law?)
- Whether Carioca's Listing was made in 1993 or 1994.
- Whether the Entry Sign provision was for Langley or Verde Hospitality.
- Whether Dick Pogue was licensed with Carioca's agent/broker Montezuma Land Co. January 3, 1993.
- Whether Brown's denial of neglect of duty is a disputed issue of fact.

- Whether Carioca's survey of its property was made in January or December 1994. Was it made for Verde Hospitality or for Langley?
- Whether Carioca's misrepresentation of its survey and sign are in genuine dispute.
- Whether Carioca's buyer Verde Hospitality was created as a lawful entity before September 1994.

These issues in dispute relate to the claims. Fact-finding was required to resolve the genuine issues before the U.S. District Court. Genuine issues of dispute in abuse of process and legal malpractice, stated and meritorious, were not decided pursuant to law.

Summary judgment should have been denied the defendants.

Some of the unsettled disputes stand independent of decisions made in state court. The district court failed in its duty.

Judge Broomfield's errors of law formed the basis for appeal to the Ninth Circuit. Simply put, a jury was to be given the disputed issues of fact and allowed to make the determinations in favor of one side or the other.

Apparently Broomfield did not trust a jury to reach the same conclusion that he did.

It appears that in closing the case Broomfield had, in his mind at least, shut the door on another disfavored action in the good old boy network in Arizona.

For the sake of redundancy, Judge Broomfield was not permitted to reach a factual conclusion. Regardless, he weighed the evidence and made factual determinations, without lawful authority to do so.

Immune System

The Court's Way Out

Suppression of meritorious claims is typically the result of some form of corruption or incompetence. Corruption is the more complex of the two but the result is usually the same, a miscarriage, the law dishonored.

In our courts, a judge may uphold another judge's ruling, not because it was legally correct, but just because of protocol, albeit wrong. Permit a poor analogy. A bird-dog makes a false point. Another backs him up; not because a bird is there, but just because he wants to honor the other dog's point. I hesitate to call it bird-dog protocol, but I think you get the point. Pun intended.

While I was moving for determination of fact and for disclosure in federal court the defendants were pleading with Broomfield to deny the evidence and obscure the facts. In cooperation with the attorneys federal judge Broomfield muddied the course with false inferences of fact. Finally, Broomfield's outright misstatements of fact supported the injustice that became programmed and ordered in his court.

Malpractice is not complex. The plaintiff must demonstrate, and prove at trial, an attorney-client relationship, duty, breach, injury and damages. With the exception of the first element, relationship, the claim is the same as negligence. The same standards are applied. To be successful in a claim, the plaintiff must convince the trier of fact of his attorney's legal negligence, and that he caused his damages. Where a jury is present it is in their domain to decide the factual issues. The judge in such instance may only apply the law; in this case the law of Arizona, to the claim of legal malpractice.

The factual issues in dispute with defendant Brown over the malpractice claim is little trouble to decide. In state court Judge Lindbergh had already decided that Brown was negligent. Brown's relationship to me and his duty were not disputed. Broomfield was faced only with the issues of causation and damages in the malpractice suit.

"The court recognized the genuine issue of proximate cause in its order. BER p58 ln6. However the court in the next paragraph attempted to transfer Brown's burden in his motion for summary judgment to Langley. BER p58 ln8. The district court without discretion to do so assumed the role of jury in deciding the issue of causation in the claim of legal malpractice. [Langley Br., 10ff]." (From Langley's Reply Brief on appeal. "BER" is Brown's Excerpts of Record.)

Since both cause and damages are issues of fact, Broomfield needed only refer the matter to a jury for factual determination. Rather than do this however, Broomfield attempted to weigh the evidence. Further, he drew inferences of fact and made false determination of fact, acts prohibited under summary motion.

By settled law Judge Broomfield was barred from weighing fact and making inference of fact. On this issue there is no conflict between federal and Arizona law, but if there were it is apparent that federal law would prevail in a federal court.

The U.S. Supreme Court case, *Anderson v. Liberty Lobby*, is the controlling law of the land in summary judgment decision.

In what probably amounts to a judge trying to help an old friend, Broomfield went far astray of the law. He granted summary judgment to Brown that was not based upon law, or evidence. His decision, were it precedent, would destroy the law in *Anderson*. It is one of the more serious breaches of Broomfield's duty.

In an order November 21, 2002, state Judge Lindberg wrote, "The Court has concluded that the defendants herein are chargeable within the context of this case and its circumstances with their attorney's actions or failure to act." Further, the state court found the questions about Carioca's discovery violations troubling.

Demonstrating his awareness, Judge Broomfield, in his order filed February 6, 2004, wrote:

> "Certainly, if Langley believed that the Listing's date was relevant to his dispute with Carioca, he could have so argued in the Carioca Litigation. Even though he did not do so, it was his attorney that disclosed the document in that case; hence, he clearly had possession of it."

Brown, you will recall, failed to do discovery on

the Listing. Brown's negligence, obviously, was found by U.S. District Judge Broomfield.

By Brown's own words, his declaration in the record, he never possessed the original Listing and he never knew the date it was created. Brown apparently did not know that the Listing's agent was not licensed with the Listing broker. In his late decisions Judge Broomfield, lost sight of his material finding that Brown "clearly had possession." Would Judge Broomfield go so far without considering the obvious? If Brown disclosed an incomplete or undiscovered copy would a competent court find him negligent? Why would a judge sidestep the obvious conclusion?

Expert Witness Boyd Lemon advised the court that Raymond Brown performed below a reasonable standard of care. Lemon wrote in part in his opinion for the court:

"3. Brown failed to file a Cross-Complaint against the escrow, Transamerica Title Company.

4. Brown failed to call Jack Bird as a witness at trial to show that Carioca anticipatorily breached the contract, thereby excusing Langley's performance, and to confirm that after December 31, 1993, the original closing date per the escrow instructions, the original agreement was abandoned and the parties entered into a new contract.

5. Brown's closing argument was below the standard of care in that it lacked explanation of a plausible theory under which Langley could have prevailed in the case.

It is also my opinion that but for the above acts and omissions of Brown, it is more likely than not that Langley would have had a jury verdict in his favor in the underlying action."

As an expert witness Boyd Lemon's only deficiencies may have been that he was overly qualified, and a resident of California. That said, it would appear true only in a court unduly influenced by conflict and cronyism.

In a letter to Judge Janis Sterling, November 16, 1995, Brown admitted his ineffectiveness and requested leniency. In fact Brown proposed that the court order sanctions or penalty against himself rather than his client. At the time, I was his client.

The State Bar of Arizona found Brown four years later, after extended petition and response, in breach of professional responsibilities. In the Bar's file Number 99-1135 Brown was formally reprimanded and referred to the Bar's diversion program. The penalty, I believe, was inadequate. Too often too much damage is done by an attorney neglecting his duty to a client. Ask anyone that has been there and they will probably tell you that the "time does not fit the crime."

The record in Broomfield's court demonstrates the negligence of Raymond Brown. In a reasonable examination Brown's legal negligence is obvious. The remaining issues of causation and damages could only be, must be, decided by the trier of fact-- a jury.

What are the scenarios under which a federal judge would stare the evidence in the face and deny its existence? I believe the decision of the Ninth

Circuit will help answer that question.

In the meantime, a layman's analysis: It appears that Broomfield somewhere along the way ceased being a judge. Again, the question is why? Although he was empowered to make decision and orders, he apparently lost his way. In reaching out to help conclude the case, or aid his fellow attorneys, he took the role of jury. Improper and unlawful, he made decisions that he was prohibited from making, and that could only be made by the authority of a duly impaneled jury.

Errors of Law

J udge Broomfield made both law and factual error. Factual errors are not always so obvious. I believe errors of law are more so.

Judges are supposed to decide issues of law holding to principles of settled cases and higher court decision. Appellate courts usually refrain from deciding issues of fact since that is the domain of the trier, the jury or the judge, as may be applicable.

The record in Broomfield's court herein establishes each of the matters.

It seems reasonable, I believe, to concentrate on the issues of appeal concerned with the law of the case. It should be noted though, that when a judge grants a summary judgment motion, his decision is reviewable *de novo*. Under the *de novo* standard the appeals court is supposed to examine matters of both fact and law using a trial court's standard.

Broomfield's errors of law in 0497 conflict with:

- The law of *Anderson* which provides that the weighing and inferring of fact is prohibited at the summary judgment phase. Broomfield broke the settled law of the U.S. Supreme Court. Broomfield disqualified himself by granting summary judgment in the negligence claim after he had found causation an issue. His decision is contrary to findings of neglect by himself and others, as well as the admitted genuine issues over the elements of causation and damages.

- The law of Arizona, *Collins v. Miller & Miller; Phillips v. Clancy; Boozer v. Arizona Country Club*, provides that causation is an issue of fact that must be decided by the finder of fact—a jury in this case. Broomfield weighed the genuine issue of causation and inferred certain fact. Broomfield abused judicial discretion by assuming the role of jury.

And, more specifically:

- Broomfield ignored briefings and applicable federal law that imposed a duty to use the substantive law of Arizona in this diversity of citizenship action.

- Broomfield decided that the defendants' abuse of process could not be brought in his court. His decision is in direct conflict with the applicable law of Arizona that holds a party or attorney may abuse process while defending a claim. For further information see, *Nienstedt v. Wetzel; Morn v. City of Phoenix; Crackel v. Allstate Insurance Company*.

- Broomfield abused discretion by denying petition to find fact. His decision to prevent complete discovery, and to allow moving discovery, solicited defendant falsehoods. Judge Broomfield failed to examine the evidence that demonstrates ill motive and intent by the defendant parties and their counsel.

The major arena for error is in the body of law that was applied to the case by Broomfield. The circuit panel, under appeal, should focus upon these substantive errors of law.

In district court Judge Broomfield had three choices. Two of the three would be based in error. First, the court could misapply the appropriate substantive law. Error in the first part is easily done and easily detected. The judge merely cites appropriate cases, but makes erroneous application. In the second choice, the court could find law that is inapplicable under the diversity standard and apply it. The law in the second instance would likely come from non-forum states. In instances of conflict, the law of other states would not be applicable. Finally, in the third choice the court could apply the appropriate law available to it. The substantive law of Arizona, the law of the case, would meet that need.

Judge-made error, especially errors of law that are plain to see, should be corrected upon appeal. Fully briefed, an appeals court has a right or wrong decision. Simply put there are clear choices, and a court that divests itself of judicial duty must be more deliberative in its reasoning, more cunning in distancing itself from applicable law.

To aid the court all parties filed briefs, giving Broomfield the benefit of argument and case law.

In spite of his consideration, or lack thereof, Judge Broomfield failed to apply the law of the case.

He apparently failed to consider *Boozer v. Arizona Country Club* and *Collins v. Miller & Miller*, substantive law in the malpractice claim; as well as *Morn v. City of Phoenix*, in the abuse of process claim; all substantive law of Arizona.

Crackel, et al v. Allstate Insurance Company, was filed in Division Two, Arizona Court of Appeals about the time my appeal was being made to the Ninth Circuit. *Crackel*, not untimely for the Circuit Court, gives support to the other applicable Arizona cases, and further defines misuse of legal process in Arizona.

Broomfield did not use the settled law of Arizona. Instead, he relied upon the law of non-forum states, citing cases out of California, Virginia, Alabama, and New York.

The Carioca defendants weighed in with more deception, and Brown cited inapplicable law from non-forum states. The district court used Brown's citations, almost without exception.

Although Broomfield cited applicable federal law, including *Anderson* for summary judgment decision, he did not apply obligatory and significant federal law to the case. The errors are rather easy to understand but a more thorough examination is due.

Further, impropriety and the conflict that should have caused Judge Broomfield to disqualify himself need review. Broomfield's decisions should be examined, as well as his prospective motives. The role of the Judicial Council of the Ninth Circuit Court and its position are to be addressed.

In these matters the appearance of prejudice is examined, objectively, although it may not appear to be in a light favorable to Judge Broomfield. I hope to give the benefit of doubt where there is doubt, while refusing to shy away from corruption or incompetence where there can be no doubt.

Immune System

The Evidence of Impropriety

The Judge's role in a case with jury demand is to decide issues of law. If there is dispute among the parties as to law, the court will be briefed, take the matter under advisement, read the applicable law and issue its decision. In theory, if not in practice, a judge's errors of law, if any, will be corrected or overturned on appeal to a higher court.

There can be little question about a judge's authority to issue a decision from the bench. His authority, however, apparently ends where the law is no longer a basis for his decision.

In the summary judgment decision Broomfield could not weigh the evidence, find or infer fact. Under authority, he could decide and apply the substantive law of Arizona to settle legal argument. And, he could decide and apply settled federal law applicable to summary decision, under clear standards that were plainly before him.

At the summary judgment phase the jury demand prohibits the judge from deciding fact. If a dispute is found the judge must make the call whether it is a genuine issue. He can go no farther in his deliberation.

In granting defendants summary judgment

Broomfield wrote lengthy, laborious orders. Defendant Brown in his Appellate Brief referred to, ". . .the district court's painstaking determinations."

Broomfield went into detail in his analysis of the Real Estate Listing, as well as the issue of cause in the negligence claim. What reasons other than genuine dispute would Broomfield have had for such examination of the evidence? Obviously those issues as well as others he analyzed were genuine, and in dispute. Thus each of Judge Broomfield's efforts to weigh the evidence and then to infer or determine fact establishes cause to overturn his decision on appeal.

The merits of the appeal are shown in Broomfield's deliberations. His disregard of and conflict with the settled law of *Anderson v. Liberty Lobby* is clear and convincing. Did Judge Broomfield examine Arizona law? *Boozer*, *Phillips*, and *Collins* make clear that negligence (malpractice) claims are not suited for summary judgment, and in the case before him could not be granted lawfully. Regardless, Broomfield granted all the defendants his favor in summary motions.

A standard of proof could not enter into the equation for Judge Broomfield.

In his order Judge Broomfield wrote, citing *Phillips* in *Glaze v. Larsen*.

"As with all negligence claims, a plaintiff asserting legal malpractice must prove the existence of a duty, breach of duty, that the defendants' negligence was the actual and proximate cause of injury ~."

There it is again. Did you see it? The fact finder's standard, "must prove" in the first sentence.

Broomfield went on to write more about proof and proximate cause, matters of which he possessed little or no discretion; violations of duty imposed by *Anderson, Boozer, Phillips,* and *Collins.*

The law of *Collins* was totally missing in Broomfield's analysis.

Broomfield's decisions were judiciously unsound, and prejudiced in favor of the defendants/movants.

The proper discretionary standard imposed a duty upon Judge Broomfield to allow the jury to decide the disputed and uncertain facts about the Listing, and apply those findings in its verdict. Broomfield noted his duty in a prior order when he wrote: "At the time of trial, the jury will determine any relevant facts which are of consequence to the determination of the claims advanced in this case."

A question for those who need to know is whether Broomfield delegated the final decision to a clerk, or wrote the order himself. Of course, in either event Broomfield remains responsible.

There are too many errors in Judge Broomfield's recent orders to be mere oversight. For a judge to make so many blunders he would have to have been under a spell of some kind. For a moment just review: Broomfield ignored all the findings of Raymond Brown's neglect. Broomfield abused discretion by disregarding the applicable federal law and the law of Arizona, the forum state; as well as critical matters of summary judgment, including standards of proof, the genuine dispute over causation, false inferences of fact, and the weighing of evidence.

Broomfield weighed the evidence and inferred fact in the issue of causation that was reserved explicitly for a jury.

Broomfield decided that evidence of misuse of process could not be brought in his court in direct confrontation with existing law. Further, Broomfield refused to examine the motive and intent of defendants in acts of deception and direct falsehood.

I discovered after my claims were dismissed under summary judgment that the same law firm representing Defendant Carioca was representing U.S. District Judge Robert C. Broomfield. It is more likely than not that the judge was under the influence of conflict or prejudice. Either the judge or the defendant made no disclosure of notice of conflict. Judge Broomfield's Financial Disclosure included the pages that follow. Certain other public records are also included in Images 3 through 8. Carioca's counsel is named on Image 6 of the series.

In granting defendant motions, it is without question that Judge Broomfield ruled in favor of attorneys and parties with whom he does business. The integrity of the judicial process was breached. It cannot be determined accident or mere oversight that a federal judge breaches his duty, disregards settled law, and misuses his power to aid those whose favors he seeks.

Clearly the law and the evidence supported my subsequent pursuit of due process. The circumstances under which meritorious claims of legal malpractice and abuse of process were disposed of require examination.

My inquiry began with a single click of the

mouse. It seemed there was little choice as more clicks turned up more and more evidence of judicial impropriety. Broomfield was one of the investors in a Bell Grande partnership. The state of Arizona reports that Bell Grande's statutory agent at the time relevant was David L. Lansky of Mariscal, Weeks, McIntyre & Friedlander, P.A., the firm that represents my opponent, The Carioca Company. Broomfield reported in his personal disclosure that he owned interests in the Bell Grande partnerships. The Bell Grande investments are shown on Image 5 in the series that begins with the next page.

United States District Court
District of Arizona
Sandra Day O'Connor United States Courthouse
Phoenix, Arizona 85003

Chambers of
Robert C. Broomfield
Senior United States District Judge

RECEIVED

'00? AUG - : A I'?

FINANCIAL 2004
DISCLOSURE OFFICE

Hon. Mary M. Lisi, Chair
Committee on Financial Disclosure
Suite 2-301
One Columbus Circle, N.E.
Washington, D.C. 20544

Dear Judge Lisi:

With regard to your letter of July 2, 2004, this letter is
intended as a response and amendment to my 2003 Financial
Disclosure Report. I list the responses in the order in which
you list them in your letter.

As to Part VII, page 1, line 8, this probably could fairly
be considered a gift from ▓▓▓▓▓▓▓▓ but I prefer to include
it in Column D. It is a ▓▓▓▓ tenancy interest acquired on
October 22, 2003 from ▓▓▓▓▓▓▓▓▓ with a code value of K
and a gain code of A.

As to Part VII, page 1, line 7, this account was mistakenly
included. It should have been listed as a part of number 3 (see
instructions page 37, number 2, second bullet).

As to Part VII, page 1, line 2, the sale was to Allen L. and
Emily S. Lacy, husband and wife.

As to Part VII, page 1, line 2 and page 2, line 36, the
Farmland - McClain County, OK was entirely disposed of on October
1, 2003 as noted in the preceding paragraph. The code value for
Column D(3) is N. The Mobile Mini, Inc. in Trust #2 was entirely
disposed of and the code value was listed in Column D(3).

As to Part VII, page 1, line 2, Column C(2) the Farmland -
McClain County, OK listed the value code as "T" because it was
sold for cash. Since there was an appraisal for the buyer's
financing purposes, I guess "Q" is as good as anything so I'll
use it even though "T" seems more accurate.

Judicial Complaint Exhibit C

Image 3
The Letter From Judge Robert C. Broomfield, Redacted by Others

July26, 2004
Page Two

    As to Part VII, page 1, line 8, Column C(2), as I have indicated above, the appraisal was obtained by the buyer. We do not have a copy of it (nor were we entitled to one) and we think it was obtained some time in September or October, 2003.

    As you requested, two additional copies of this response are attached.

RCB:lp
Enclosures

Image 4
Page Two of the Letter from Judge Robert C.
Broomfield, Redacted by Others

| FINANCIAL DISCLOSURE REPORT
Page 1 of 3 | Name of Person Reporting
Broomfield, Robert C | | Date of Report
3/3/2004 |

VII. INVESTMENTS and TRUSTS — income, value, transactions (includes those of the spouse and dependent children. See pp. 34-57 of filing instructions.)

A. Description of Assets (including trust assets) Place "(X)" after each asset exempt from prior disclosure	B. Income during reporting period		C. Gross value at end of reporting period		D. Transactions during reporting period				
	(1) Amount Code 1 (A-H)	(2) Type (e.g. div, rent, or int.)	(1) Value Code 2 (J-P)	(2) Value Method Code 3 (Q-W)	(1) Type (e.g. buy, sell, merger, redemption)	(2) Date Month-Day	(3) Value Code 2 (J-P)	(4) Gain Code 1 (A-H)	(5) Identity of buyer/seller (if private transaction)
☐ NONE (No reportable income, assets, or transactions)									
1. Farmland - McClain County, OK	C	Rent	N	W					
2. Farmland - McClain County, OK		None	N	T	sale	10/1	N	Q	
3. Wells Fargo Money Market, Phoenix, AZ	A	Interest	N	T					
4. Pruco Life Variable Appreciable Policy	C	cash value line	K	T					
5. Mineral Interests - Grady County, OK		None	J	W					
6. Mineral Interests - Stephens County, OK		None	J	W					
7. Wells Fargo Bank - money market, Phoenix, AZ	A	Interest	J	T					
8. Investment Property - Phoenix, AZ	A	Rent	L	Q					
9. I am successor trustee of Trust #2 having following assets:		-							
10. Arizona Business Bank - Cash and two CD's	E	Interest	P1	T					
11. Interest in Bell Grande Limited Partnership, Scottsdale, AZ	F	Distribution	O	W					
12. Interest in Bell Grande II Ltd Partnership, Scottsdale, AZ	G	Distribution	O	W					
13. Interest in Val Vista & W.F.Rd. LtdPartnership, Scottsdale, AZ		None	O	W					
14. Interest in Suncrest at RMI Ltd Partnership, Phoenix, AZ	B	Distribution	K	W					
15. House and lot - Phoenix, AZ		None	O	Q					
16. Furniture and Furnishings at previously listed asset		None	J	W					
17. COBIZ-Colorado Business Bank - common stock	C	Dividend	O	T					
18. Great Hall Investment Funds	A	Dividend	O	T					

1. Income/Gain Codes: A = $1,000 or less B = $1,001-$2,500 C = $2,501-$5,000 D = $5,001-$15,000 E = $15,001-$50,000
   (See Columns B1 and D4) F = $50,001-$100,000 G = $100,001-$1,000,000 H1 = $1,000,001-$5,000,000 H2 = More than $5,000,000
2. Value Codes: J = $15,000 or less K = $15,001-$50,000 L = $50,001-$100,000 M = $100,001-$250,000
   (See Columns C1 and D3) N = $250,000-$500,000 O = $500,001-$1,000,000 P1 = $1,000,001-$5,000,000 P2 = $5,000,001-$25,000,000
   P3 = $25,000,001-$50,000,000 P4 = More than $50,000,000
3. Value Method Codes: Q = Appraisal R = Cost (Real Estate Only) S = Assessment T = Cash/Market
   (See Column C2) U = Book Value V = Other W = Estimated

Image 5
A Page From Judge Broomfield's Financial Disclosure Showing an Interest in the Bell Grande Partnerships at lines 11 and 12.

Arizona Corporation Commission
State of Arizona Public Access System

04/03/2005   11:54 AM

File Number: L-0946594-3
Corp. Name: BELL GRANDE II, L.C.

Domestic Address

15170 N HAYDEN RD
SCOTTSDALE, AZ 85260

Statutory Agent Information

Agent Name: DAVID L LANSKY

Agent Mailing/Physical Address:
% MARISCAL WEEKS MCINTYRE & FRI
2901 N CENTRAL AVE #200
PHOENIX, AZ 85012

Agent Status: APPOINTED 04/13/2000
Agent Last Updated:

Officer and Director Information

Name:	BELL GRANDE LC
Title:	MEMBER
Address:	15170 N HAYDEN RD #2
	SCOTTSDALE, AZ 85260
Date Assigned: 04/13/2000	Last Updated: 05/08/2000

Additional Corporate Information

	Corporation Type: DOMESTIC L.L.C.
Incorporation Date: 04/13/2000	Corporate Life Period: PERPETUAL
Domicile: ARIZONA	County: MARICOPA
Approval Date: 04/13/2000	Original Publish Date:

Annual Reports

No Annual Reports on File

Judicial Complaint Exhibit A
http://starpas.cc.state.az.us/cgi-bin/wspd_cgi.sh/WService=wsbroker1/names-detail.p?name-id=L09...   04/03/05

Image 6
A Document From the Arizona Corporation
Commission Showing Mariscal Weeks McIntyre &
Fri [Friedlander] as Agents for Bell Grande LC,
Bearing Corporate Name of Belle Grande II, L.C.

Unofficial
Document

When Recorded, Mail to:

David Lansky, Esq.
Mariscal, Weeks, McIntyre & Friedlander
2901 North Central Avenue
Suite 200
Phoenix, AZ 85012-2705

_____ REPURCHASE AGREEMENT

THIS REPURCHASE AGREEMENT (this "Agreement") is made and entered into this as of the _____ day of _____, 2001, by and between BELL GRANDE II, L.L.C. an Arizona limited liability company ("Bell Grande"), and LOWE'S HIW, Inc., a Washington corporation ("Buyer").

FIRST AMERICAN TITLE   W I T N E S S E T H :

THAT WHEREAS, Lowe's and Bell Grande has entered into that certain Agreement to Sell and Purchase Real Estate (the "Purchase Agreement"), whereby Lowe's purchased those certain premises from Bell Grande more particularly described on Exhibit "A" attached hereto and incorporated herein by reference (the "Lowe's Property"); and

WHEREAS, Bell Grande will continue to own property adjacent to the Lowe's Property which property is more particularly described on Exhibit "B" attached hereto and incorporated herein by reference (the "Bell Grande Property"); and

WHEREAS, the Lowe's Property and the Bell Grande Property are part of a shopping center (the "Shopping Center") which is depicted on Exhibit "C" attached hereto and incorporated herein by reference; and

WHEREAS, as part of the Purchase Agreement, the parties agreed to provide Bell Grande the right to repurchase the Lowe's Property subject to the terms and conditions of this Agreement.

NOW, THEREFORE, for and in consideration of the mutual covenants and conditions contained herein, the sufficiency of which consideration is acknowledged by all parties hereto, IT IS HEREBY AGREED AS FOLLOWS:

1.   Purchase Period

http://156.42.40.50/UnOfficialDocs/new/20010365619_1.png

Image 7
An Unofficial Recorded Document Bearing the Name of Bell Grande and Mariscal Weeks

Page 1 of 1

20010365619

State of Arizona)
) ss.
County of Maricopa)

The foregoing instrument was acknowledged before me this 27th day of April, 2001, by Warner A. Gabel, III, the President of CC&G Strategic Investments, LC the Manager of Bell Grande, L.C., an Arizona limited liability company, the sole member of Bell Grande II, L.C., an Arizona limited liability company, on behalf of the company.

My Commission Expires:

http://156.42.40.50/UnOfficialDocs/new/20010365619_11.png 04/04/05

Image 8
Evidence of Recorded Instrument Bearing Name of Bell Grande II, L.C.

Is it necessary under rule of law to know whether Broomfield had a disqualifying conflict? Apparently not. In the federal standard, the appearance of impropriety (conflict more likely than not) is sufficient. It would not be necessary to know the extent of his conflict.

Was there conflict that would disqualify Judge Broomfield? A federal judge following the canons of conduct would have recused himself. Without Judicial Watch and the empowerment of the Internet how would I have known.

Broomfield's Bell Grande Connection

Who are Broomfield's partners in the Bell Grande investment? Are they members of the law firm that represents both he and Carioca? Or, are they owners of Carioca? We may never know--the record does not show this information. In a true judicial sense, however, it is not necessary to know. The appearance of impropriety is sufficient to disqualify a judge from hearing a case.

Judge Broomfield acted without or in spite of any concern for the rule of judicial conduct. Broomfield acted without concern for the appearance of impropriety; and possibly without concern for a disqualifying conflict of interest. Furthermore, Broomfield gave no warning in the case. There was no chance to give a vote of confidence. Regardless, Broomfield entered summary judgment decisions that were clearly in conflict with fact and law in favor of Carioca and its associated defendants.

Impropriety remains relevant to present status

and any post-appeal action, even though learned too late to impact Broomfield's summary decisions.

It is the duty of the chief judge, or the judicial council of the Ninth Circuit, to order an investigation of Judge Broomfield. A misconduct complaint in proper order was put before the Judicial Council of the U.S. Ninth Circuit Court. An investigation could determine the extent of Broomfield's involvement with defendants or their counsel.

In view of the evidence, documented and made of record in the circuit, an investigation should have followed. Judge Broomfield's personal investments could involve parties, as well as attorneys, in the subject case.

It is evident that a standard of proof was not required at the time. The mere appearance of prejudice is sufficient. Other responsible judges and competent courts have rendered their decisions. They are found in the settled law of this country. In an ethical environment the evidence is compelling.

"The relevant federal statute, 28 U.S.C. § 455(a), provides that 'any justice, judge, or magistrate judge of the United States shall disqualify himself in any proceeding in which his impartiality might reasonably be questioned.' 28 U.S.C. § 455(a). The Supreme Court has stated that the purpose of this provision is 'to promote public confidence in the integrity of the judicial process.' *Liljeberg v. Health Servs. Acquisition Corp.*, 486 U.S. 847, 860, 100 L. Ed. 2d 855, 108 S. Ct. 2194 (1988)."

The law, if adhered to, rendered Judge

Broomfield unfit to make an order or judgment in this case. The appearance of impropriety casts doubt over all of Judge Broomfield's decisions, even those that are indirectly related. Recusal or disqualification was appropriate. His decisions are tainted and appear to be void or voidable. Whitewash will not work.

"We have previously stated that the 'public's confidence in the judiciary . . . may be irreparably harmed if a case is allowed to proceed before a judge who appears to be tainted.' *In re Kensington Int'l Ltd.*, 353 F.3d 211, 220 (3d Cir. 2003)."

The court's have further clarified their intent. Apparently, even in cases in which the facts were unknown and objection not made.

"We may overlook the failure to object where the 'error seriously affects the fairness, integrity or public reputation of judicial proceedings.' *United States v. Olano*, 507 U.S. 725, 732, 123 L. Ed. 2d 508, 113 S. Ct. 1770 (1993)."

There were two of the judicial council members that disqualified themselves from ruling on the evidence of Broomfield's impropriety. They were both judges of the federal court in Arizona. There were no judges from my home state, Nevada, selected for the Judicial Council of the Ninth Circuit.

Why did the Arizona district judges recuse themselves? Did they know something the others didn't? Or were they rightfully concerned with the appearance of prejudice that might result from being housed and associated with Judge

Broomfield; if they cast a ballot. Given this possibility, it is interesting that the Arizona members of the council were more respectful of the rules of judicial conduct than was Senior Judge Robert C. Broomfield.

"The gist of the tort is the misuse of the power of the court: It is an act done under the authority of the court for the purpose of perpetrating an injustice, i.e., a perversion of the judicial process to the accomplishment of an improper purpose." Twyford v. Twyford, 63 Cal. App. 3d 916, 134 Cal. Rptr. 145 (Cal.App.Dist.3 11/05/1976).

PART 3:

Trumping Due Process

Dignifying Error

Judge Broomfield wrote in his order of June 14, 2004 that my petition to reverse or vacate his judgment was without merit. Broomfield chose to classify my motion as one for reconsideration, saying that such a motion can be determined under either Rule 59(e) or 60(b). In his concluding remarks he wrote that Langley "has certainly not demonstrated that the court acted outside its authority."

It seems Broomfield was saying that he gets a free pass if his errors were made with authority, perhaps even if they were deliberate.

To err is human, but error disregarded is not judicial. The mark of a judge therefore should not be the number of errors made but the number he corrects.

Will the panel of appellate judges abandon duty in deference to the limits of Broomfield's authority?

Could it be that after issuing his decision Judge Broomfield did not seriously consider any of my pleadings? Was it his plan to add to the defendants' cover?

Chief Judge Mary Schroeder of the Ninth

Circuit denied my petition for investigation into Broomfield's improprieties; unwilling, it seemed, to examine the evidence of alternative reasons for his decisions. Claiming that I had not met my burden, Judge Schroeder wrote, "Furthermore, although complainant submitted certain exhibits, he failed to provide any objectively verifiable proof (for example, names of witnesses, recorded documents, or transcripts) supporting his allegation of a conflict of interest."

It appears the Chief Judge was protecting Judge Broomfield's backside. Had she failed to consider the recorded documents that were submitted as exhibits? The documents (public records bearing proof) made available to Judge Schroeder are copied and included herein. Images 3 through 8 are found following page 69.

Judge Schroeder too, it seems, forgot that the mere appearance of impropriety is sufficient to sustain the claim against Judge Broomfield.

Writing at page 2 of the order, Judge Schroeder said, "Complainant's case is on appeal. His exhibits, as well as the docket sheets in the district court and circuit court, have been carefully reviewed."

She wrote in the order that "Even multiple or very wrong legal decisions may be addressed under the ordinary course of appellate review."

Under the *de novo* standard, the errors of law and fact should be examined and corrected.

Other than the review of the docket and exhibits, I had not been given any notice of any reading of the briefs that were filed. Judge Schroeder's writings were obviously pointed to the case under appeal and not the complaint against

Judge Broomfield.

Judge Schroeder wrote her decision in August 2005. The last brief was filed January 3, 2005. Naturally, I would like to have the appellate decision to examine and comment on now.

Schroeder's order says the complaint (against Broomfield) relates to a number of the judge's rulings and decisions in complainant's civil case. The case was already under appeal when I discovered the evidence of Judge Broomfield's impropriety. However, as noted in the previous chapter, even the failure to object can be overlooked, under law.

Judge Schroeder went on to write that "A complaint will be dismissed if it is directly related to the merits of a judge's ruling or decision in the underlying case." The relationship, unavoidable perhaps, should not be grounds for dismissal. Under what circumstance would a judicial complaint be unrelated to a judge's duty? It seems to me the issues of Judge Broomfield's impropriety and conflict stand irregardless.

I believe Judge Schroeder was taking the position that prejudice and impropriety can be overlooked if the underlying case is eventually concluded under law. But, under law is operative and critical. On the one hand, if the case were not concluded under law, there would be no recourse with the judicial complaint. The process would be over with via dismissal. The cover would have worked. Broomfield would have been protected from legitimate complaint. Further, if concluded under law it would be due to the work of the circuit panel of judges. The issue of Judge Broomfield's connections and impropriety would, again, remain.

One must sit in wonder of a judicial system so out of sync with justice. It seems that error and oversight became the strong suit in Judge Schroeder's dismissal of a legitimate judicial complaint.

To her credit though, Judge Schroeder wrote that "A challenge to judge's rulings should be sought through the correct review procedure. . ." Other than appeal, I must admit that I believe I join thousands in not knowing what that procedure is. But I believe that any course taken can, and probably will, lead up a blind alley.

The order of Judge Schroeder, in judicial misconduct complaint No. 05-89056 filed August 19, 2005, was appealable within thirty days of its issue.

My judicial complaint against Judge Broomfield was based upon an obvious appearance of impropriety. I needed no reminder that his errors, separate and apart, were to be reviewed under appeal to the Ninth Circuit.

The Clerk and The Council

It seemed that once again the system rather than justice would prevail. The complaint against Judge Broomfield, regardless of merit, had not been given legs.

I called the clerk's office, Ninth Circuit October 17, 2005, to inquire about the status of my petition for review of Judge Schroeder's order. After being transferred to a non-English speaking fax machine I hung up, then called back. Connected with a live being, I was told I was speaking to Alex.

Alex told me his supervisor, Robin Donoghue, could talk to me about the complaint pending review by the judicial council. Robin, however, was out of the office.

Alex took my number and said he would give Robin a note to call me the next day.

Robin did not call the next day. Strange as it appears, though; an unsigned order was entered by the clerk that same day, October 17, 2005. And a cover letter, signed by Clerk Cathy A. Catterson, also dated October 17, 2005, reminded me that law provided for no further review of the complaint against Judge Broomfield. The unsigned single-page order was, presumably, on behalf of the Ninth Circuit Judicial Council.

I did eventually hear from Robin. I received a letter from her dated January 18, 2006, about another matter. In the last stages of this writing, I decided I should contact Ms. Donoghue again, to review the unlikely events of October 17, 2005.

In a letter of June 16, 2006, I wrote:

"I made a phone call to the Ninth Circuit Clerk's office October 17, 2005. I wanted to learn the status of the judicial complaint I had filed against Judge Robert C. Broomfield, assigned Docket Number 05-89056. The person I spoke with, identifying himself as Alex, told me that you could speak to me about the matter. My call was transferred to a fax answering machine. After calling back, I was told that you were out of the office that day. I was assured that you would receive a message to call me the next day.

Instead of your call, I received an order a few days later that was dated that same day, October 17, 2005, with cover letter of same date from Clerk Cathy Catterson. The single page Order, unsigned, bears only a date stamp. The time it was filed is unknown to me.

Questions arise that I feel should be addressed. Did you receive a message to call me on October 18, 2005? Who prepared the order that was filed October 17, 2005? Did all 12 [sic] members of the judicial council review the Order, and my Complaint? Ms. Donoghue can you tell me how likely it is that due process materialized between the time of my phone call and the filing of the order on that single day of October 17, 2005."

In her reply dated June 19, 2006, Ms. Donoghue wrote:

"In response to your letter to me dated June 16, at this point I honestly cannot recall whether I received a telephone message from you on or about October 18, 2005. However, processing of judicial misconduct complaints and petitions for review is handled by the Clerk's Office. The form of Order used by the Judicial Council affirming dismissals customarily is unsigned and date-stamped, and the complaint file and Order are sent to all members of the Judicial Council entitled to vote on petitions for review.

Any further inquiries regarding your complaint should be directed to the attention of the Clerk's Office."

Key questions were not answered by Ms. Donoghue. Her reply raised additional issues. Who decided on the form of Order that was sent to all members of the Judicial Council entitled to vote? Did due process materialize? How likely is it that any member initiated the order?

Does it remind you of the circle of life? Does it begin and end with the Clerk? With nothing of substance in between?

In the phase of judicial complaint, the ninth circuit judicial council comprised of 10 selected judges, took the same position as Judge Schroeder. In their words, they saw no reason to change Judge Schroeder's order.

Error and oversight were confirmed. In the

Council's unsigned order filed October 17, 2005, it is stated, "For the reasons stated by the Chief Judge and based upon the controlling authority cited in support thereof, we affirm."

The deal was done. Cathy Catterson, Clerk of the Ninth Circuit, wrote in her cover letter October 17, 2005, that. . ."no further review of this complaint is provided for by law."

Judges Stephen M. McNamee and Roger G. Strand, members of the council from the district court of Arizona, did not participate in the consideration of the judicial complaint. There were no judges from my home state of Nevada that were assigned to the council.

The judicial council was comprised of the following judges:

Arthur L. Alarcon, Senior Ninth Circuit Judge, Carter appointment 1979;

Alex Kozinski, Ninth Circuit Judge, Reagan appointment 1985;

Andrew J. Kleinfield, Circuit Judge, Bush appointment 1991;

Kim McLane Wardlaw, Circuit Judge, Clinton appointment, 1995-98;

William A. Fletcher, Circuit Judge, Clinton appointment 1997;

Stephen M. McNamee, Chief District Judge, Arizona, Bush appointment 1990;

Roger G. Strand, Senior District Judge, Arizona, Reagan appointment 1985;

David Alan Ezra, Chief District Judge, Hawaii, Reagan appointment 1988;

David F. Levi, District Judge, California, Bush appointment 1990;

B. Lynn Winmill, District Judge, Idaho, Clinton appointment 1995.

The list appears to be politically neutral. Four appointments by Democrats and six by Republicans, with two GOP appointments not voting, leaving a 4 to 4 split.

Did the panel protect a fellow judge?

Indifference or corruption, it must be said, has no political affiliation.

I cannot help but be amazed at the series of events. Questions of procedure, rule, intent and compliance enter the picture. Was the one-page order hurriedly prepared after my phone call? Was it too late in the day to run the order by the 10 members of the judicial council? Were they all available to vote? Who directed the clerk's office to prepare and file the unsigned order in File No. 05-89056?

Meanwhile the evidence of impropriety remains. The record will not go away.

Writing in the *Las Vegas Sun* March 17, 2006, Tony Cook in "Jaded Justice" quotes an attorney critical of the state's Judicial Commission saying, "They go after politically weak judges. When there are bigoted and corrupt judges, they don't go after them because they are politically strong."

It appears, rare though it may be, that some judges are sacrificed for the sake of public opinion. But typically, merited complaint is not given proper consideration.

In an editorial appearing June 23 in the *Las Vegas Review-Journal* it is claimed that "No senior judge has ever been removed from office." Is there a special issue with senior judges? Are they more

Immune System

likely to violate the canons of judicial conduct?

Conclusion

There remains the decision on appeal. The case is made. The state and federal courts of Arizona imposed judgments built on error. Probably due more to intelligent design than blind chance.

Next, a panel of judges from the Ninth Circuit will take over the case. Unselected and untested, their *de novo* review remains to be seen.

I am anxious to review the degree to which the panel addresses the errors of district Judge Broomfield. Attorneys, finding my briefs pointing to issues, citing and arguing applicable case law with clarity, have given me positive feedback. Judge Schroeder wrote that at least a part of the record I submitted for appeal had been "carefully reviewed." That, it would seem, is positive.

If Broomfield is affirmed and his errors condoned, with little or no concern for his impropriety, then a new cause of action surfaces. The "search" would go on. In district court claims for denial of meaningful access to the courts and malicious abuse of process would be appropriate. Demand for declaratory judgment to clarify issues of substantive law would be made. I believe it would then be necessary to name Judge Robert C.

Broomfield a defendant, at least in his official capacity.

Judge Broomfield was not given law-making powers; that's a role enjoyed by legislative bodies. Legal precedent provides the framework for a judge to find the law of a case.

In the best of circumstances, that is where a claim is not opposed by the good 'ol boy network, a case that goes to appeal has less than a 5% chance of remand or reversal. It seems to me that it is in the making of this statistic that appellate courts are most deficient. Merited complaints and petitions are frequently buried with unlawful decisions. With machine like precision too many appellate opinions are stamped out by circuit courts with the "NOT FOR PUBLICATION" designation; reason and merit discarded.

Can the honest and competent element of the profession benefit from the shysters shuffle? Obviously half the litigants lose in any case. Attorneys, contentious or threatened are quick to quote the statistic.

Pressured to win their cases attorneys often twist the law, or use bad law to make an argument. It is generally known that the *pro per* is discriminated against. Therefore even if he uses applicable law and proper argument, the court may unfairly favor his law-schooled opponent.

As I began the task of writing the book, I considered the probable and possible views of my opposition. I wrote an email message to the three attorneys representing the defendants in federal court on November 22, 2005. In the message I wrote:

"The story you are familiar with is almost ready for publication. The proposed title of the book is In Search of a Court of Law, and includes a documentary account of *Langley v. Brown.*

Because you opposed my efforts to obtain justice in U.S. District Court Cause CV-00 0497 PCT RCB, I would like to invite you to present a statement for inclusion in the print version. All reasonable effort will be made to include your statement verbatim. In this regard I request that your comments and any evidentiary material be related to matters relevant to and addressed in the briefings under appeal, No. 04-16460. The book is dedicated to the public interest and all that pursue just claims. I plan to give any revenue I could receive to a university of either Arizona or Nevada and in part at least to a law school. I hope you will support this effort."

I received one response to the three messages sent. By return email Kelly Lewis of Carioca's law counsel answered with an "Out of Office AutoReply." The message had a return path of Kelly.Lewis@mwmf.com.

The message told me that Kelly was out of the office until November 11th and gave a phone number to reach his assistant, if I needed immediate assistance.

This work might be titled differently. In Search Of A Court of Law may do no justice. The Scum and the Scam might be more telling. By any other name, though, the legal profession would still be faced with its illegitimacy. The Shysters Shuffle is probably playing now, in a courtroom near you.

It is in this field of dreams that I must wait for the panel's decision. Of course if the panel reverses or remands Judge Broomfield, the matter of new claims may be moot. In this scenario a request for reconsideration to the appellate court would not be necessary. A motion would be made only if there is a need to bring new claims and to buy more time before filing.

I have often been asked why things happened. Why did the judges overlook the law and evidence? I can't explain the reasons for actions or inactions. I am interested in presenting the factual account of what happened. It strikes me, however, that no judge knows all the law. And he may not like all the law that he knows.

Pro se briefs and pleadings are disliked. The law is passed over in deference to an attorney that is oftentimes dishonest, uninformed, incompetent, or negligent. Still the courts consistently give preferential treatment to the barrister, even though he may have finished last in his class and last in the courtroom. The gristmill turns when it has feedstock. In a legal system that kowtows to power, losers are called for.

Obviously the judicial system is broken. It is unlikely that the bar associations or complacent judges will fix it. Good attorneys, and yes there are some, (they are not all dead as we might believe) fight an uphill battle.

Ultimately the responsibility and the authority to reform the judiciary rests with Congress and state legislators. Pressure must be applied by all who believe in fairness.

Many federal judges refuse to take retirement. I often wonder. Is it so they can hold power; to thwart or dismiss selected cases regardless of merit? Do they owe a lifetime debt to some former colleague? Are they there to sound the death knell for the *pro se;* indifferent perhaps and callused beyond redemption?

Able to dispel the claims of judicial misconduct and disability, these senior judges it seems are determined that no *pro se* will vindicate a fundamental right on his, or her, watch.

Crooks and their supporters need to be chased. When caught they need to be punished. I gave the chase. The record shows they were caught. The courts failed to punish. Therefore the courts bring unfavorable attention to themselves.

There is an economic side to judicial corruption. Our move to Nevada began in 1996. At first we planned to maintain our resident status in Arizona. Then, as the litigation progressed and the trial loomed, we saw more reasons to live elsewhere. It seemed Arizona was less predictable than Nevada. Over the course of trial and appeal we purchased five new automobiles, made considerable investment in home, furniture, fixtures, appliances, and paid hundreds of thousands of dollars in federal income taxes, all without paying one corresponding dime to the state of Arizona.

There is also the cost to the defendants, in pleadings and responses, for more than 260 docket items just in federal court.

Furthermore, Arizona's counterfeit courts penalize its people in hidden ways. We have placed on hold our plans to endow Arizona institutions and changed a pattern of earn and spend that will deny estate taxes and other revenues to the state. These are some of the more substantial losses Arizona has, for its tolerance of corruption in its courts. There are other indirect and less noticeable penalties to the state including loss of sales taxes and incidental and discretionary spending. And of course there's a cost to the taxpayers of Arizona to sustain the waste, aka judicial resistance to the rule of law and due process.

So who am I to blow against the wind?

I have found little that is positive with our judicial system. That goes against my nature. I am the product of an American system that taught its young to respect professionals, particularly those that wore the cloth, whether parochial or judicial.

I realize that I am joined by thousands of Americans that have been victimized by legal abuse. In a real sense, I feel I have been given an undeserved honor. One that I do not take lightly. Defending basic American rights is serious business.

There is movement in the trenches to reform, but there will be powerful opponents to change. Members of Congress are showing concern. Organizations working to empower the people and reform the legal system are using the Internet more effectively. One organization that comes to mind is WeSpeakUp.org providing space in the blogsphere at http://www.wespeakup.org /WeBlog.html. If the media gets behind them the movements will be effective.

In some states the Councils of Judicial Conduct are holding judges accountable. Elsewhere judges are being recalled for bad behavior. And those that feel the heat are sometimes resigning.

Results of the media's efforts are shown in recent investigations by the Los Angeles Times and Nevada newspapers. Corrupt practices have been exposed. Judges are being called upon to explain allegations of preferential treatment, prejudice, and judicial impropriety.

Were the judges that issued orders and judgments in my case incompetent? Were they corrupt? Yes! Which; I don't know. But in a final analysis, I doubt that it matters?

The forces that drive us have changed. News travels faster and is disseminated by a variety of media. The stories flash in front of us: "FBI Internal Investigation Expands"; "Congressman Lies"; "President Indicted"; "Judge Takes Bribe"; "Man in Custody Beaten to Death".

We have a long way to go. The present condition and the recognized trend do not speak well for our future. Arguably, whether ours is the best legal system in the world is really not the issue. If it were true then attorneys would not use the courts to abuse the American People, judicial authority would concern itself with fair hearing and due process, and in all venues Justice would not compete with connections, power and money.

Jim Brown, probably the greatest running back in football, once said his opponents tried to break him. In life as in football his opponent didn't want to destroy him, just break him. He refused to be broken.

We, with cause and will, must not be broken. The legal profession relies heavily on threats and intimidation. Those who are corrupt and connected legally, judicially, want to break their adversary. We owe a duty to ourselves and each other to not let that happen.

Afterword

I have heard it takes two to speak the truth—one to speak and another hear. Like an illness the truth must be passed on to someone.

The panel's memorandum came November 4, 2006. Filed with the clerk November 1, the *not for publication* decision of the three member panel, all senior circuit judges, affirmed the district court's grants of summary judgment.

Attorney Albert E. Van Wagner, a Pro Se defendant, submitted his bill of costs to the Ninth Circuit. In error the Clerk entered the bill on behalf of myself. The error was rendered harmless by an Order filed November 21 providing that each party bear its own costs in the appeal.

The panel did find that Judge Broomfield committed error. The panel decided the district court erred in its grant of sanctions to the defendants. The case, in part, was reversed and remanded for further consideration.

The panel in each instant wrote that Langley had "failed to submit evidence of specific facts showing that there was a genuine issue." It may be that the panel did not examine the factual content of the briefs, or the evidence included with the Excerpts of Record.

Similarly, the panel may not have known of the evidence that was submitted to the Ninth Circuit Court. Further, the panel may not have been aware of Judge Broomfield's relationship with counsel for Defendant Carioca.

It appears likely that the panel acted in spite of the evidence of specific facts.

Barely one and half pages, the memorandum did not address the issues under appeal. Errors of law and fact were not subjected to process.

The defendant's burden, in the panel's *de novo* review, escaped mention. Furthermore, the panel gave no clue that the first Rule of civil law, a just determination, was part of its agenda.

There is an inescapable irony. The district court denied my right to bring claims of abuse of process occurring in that court. Why would the circuit court expect to see evidence of specific facts in claims that were unlawfully denied? The panel's point was at least misplaced.

A second point of law that escaped consideration by the panel was the matter of Senior Judge Robert C. Broomfield's personal investment relationship with counsel for defendant/appellee The Carioca Company.

In-Text Images

REFERENCES

Substantive Law of the Case

Anderson v. Liberty Lobby, Inc., 477 U.S. 242, (1986)

Boozer v. Arizona Country Club, 434 P.2d 630, 102 Ariz. 544 (Ariz. 12/07/1967)

Collins v. Miller & Miller, 943 P.2d 747, 189 Ariz. 387, 232 Ariz. Adv. Rep. 37 (1996)

Crackel, et al v. Allstate Insurance Company, 92 P.3d 882, Ariz. App. (Div. Two, 2004)

Morn v. City of Phoenix, 152 Ariz. 164, 730 P.2d 873 (App.1986)

Nienstedt v. Wetzel, 133 Ariz. 348, 651 P.2d 876, 881 (App. 1982)

Phillips v. Clancy, 733 P.2d 300, 152 Ariz. 415 (Ariz. App.Div.1 9/11/1986)

Statutes

28 U.S.C. § 1291

28 U.S.C. §1738

Rules

Arizona District Court Rule LRCiv 83.5 (former rule 1.20)

Ninth Circuit Rule 28-1

<u>Websites</u>

www.leafmark.com   http://NJCDLP.org
www.victimsoflaw.net
www.redressinc.org   www.falseallegations.com

Virgil Langley was born in a sharecropper's shack near Searcy, Arkansas. After college in Arizona he became a teacher, and a small-time investor in real estate. He taught and served as county vocational and career education coordinator in Northern Arizona. A decade in the making, he has an appeal pending in the U.S. Ninth Circuit.

After a failed real estate transaction, Langley became the defendant in a civil action where fraud was permitted and encouraged by courts of Arizona. Virgil Langley has continued the fight for justice taking his case from the hands of unprofessional and negligent attorneys.

The legal system disfavors the likes of L a n g l e y and thwarts h i s continuing discovery of deception a n d concealment, false evidence, and judicial m i s c o n d u c t.

Langley's t r i a l attorney, once a member of the Board of Governors of The Arizona State Bar, was given formal reprimand and redirection by the bar. The damages suffered by Langley were much more severe.

There are numerous twists and legal maneuvering by the opposition as Langley seeks to have his case re-opened and then files a suit in diversity in the U.S. District Court of Arizona. Langley, a resident of Nevada, proceeds *pro se.*

www.ingramcontent.com/pod-product-compliance
Lightning Source LLC
Chambersburg PA
CBHW022001170526
45157CB00003B/1088